Eyewitness
RELIGION

Buddha head

The soul is like a charioteer
with two horses, one fine
and good and noble,
and the other the opposite

PLATO IN *PHAEDRUS* (ADAPTED)

The Greek
deities Eros,
Aphrodite, and Pan

Gemstone inscribed
with verse from
the Qur'an

To God belongs the kingdom of the
heavens and of the earth; and God
is powerful over everything

QUAR'AN IV

The mind is wavering and restless . . .
let the wise straighten their minds
as makers of arrows make their
arrows straight

GAUTAMA THE BUDDHA (ADAPTED)

Egyptian Ankh

I am all that has ever been,
I am all that is,
I am all that ever shall be,
yet never have mortal eyes
perceived me as I am

SONG TO THE EGYPTIAN MOTHER GODDESS NEIT

Christian plaque
showing Christ
on the cross

I have been born again and again,
from time to time . . . To protect
the righteous, to destroy the wicked,
and to establish the kingdom of God,
I am reborn from age to age

KRISHNA IN THE *BHAGAVAD GITA* IV

Jesus Christ is the
same yesterday and
today and for ever

HEBREWS 13:8

Statue of Hindu
avatar Krishna

Eyewitness
RELIGION

Written by
MYRTLE LANGLEY

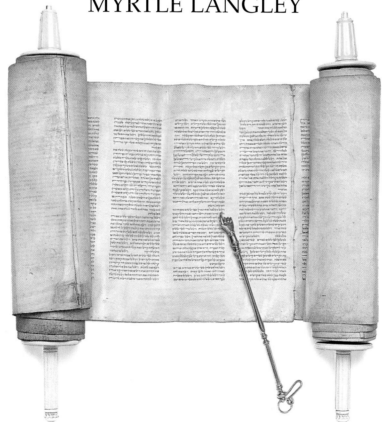

A Jewish
Torah scroll

God said to Moses, "I AM WHO I AM.
This is what you are to say to the Israelites:
'I AM has sent me to you'"

EXODUS 3: 14

DK Publishing, Inc.

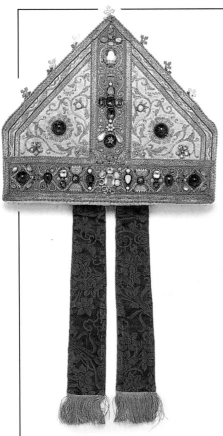

Bishop's miter

Islamic tile

LONDON, NEW YORK, MUNICH,
MELBOURNE, and DELHI

Project editor David Pickering
Art editor Sharon Spencer
Managing editor Gillian Denton
Managing art editor Julia Harris
Production Charlotte Trail
Picture research Kathy Lockley
Researcher Julie Ferris
Special photography Ellen Howden,
Andy Crawford, Geoff Dann,
Ray Moller, and Gary Ombler

REVISED EDITION
Managing editor Andrew Macintyre
Managing art editor Jane Thomas
Editor and reference compiler Lorrie Mack
Art editor Rebecca Johns
Production Jenny Jacoby
Picture research Angela Anderson
DTP designer Siu Ho

U.S. editors Elizabeth Hester, John Searcy
Publishing director Beth Sutinis
Art director Dirk Kaufman
U.S. DTP designer Milos Orlovic
U.S. production Chris Avgherinos, Ivor Parker

This Eyewitness ® Guide has been conceived by
Dorling Kindersley Limited and Editions Gallimard

This edition published in the United States in 2005
by DK Publishing, Inc.
375 Hudson Street, New York, NY 10014

05 06 07 08 09 10 9 8 7 6 5 4 3 2 1

Copyright © 1996, © 2005, Dorling Kindersley Limited

A catalog record for this book is
available from the Library of Congress.

ISBN 0-7566-1087-7 (Hardcover) 0-7566-1088-5 (Library Binding)

Color reproduction by
Colourscan, Singapore
Printed in China by Toppan Printing Co., (Shenzen) Ltd.

Discover more at
www.dk.com

Tile with writing from the Qur'an

Christian rosary
used in prayer

Hindu goddess Durga

Reclining
Buddha

Jewish Seder plate
for Passover

Tibetan
prayer
wheel

Contents

Introduction

When, as tiny babies, we first enter this world, we have no experience; we know no words; our minds are not filled with thoughts and ideas. We simply exist, aware only of our immediate surroundings and secure in the love of our parents. As we grow older we become aware of ourselves and our wider surroundings; we learn to communicate through speech as well as in other ways. Our minds and spirits are opened up to thoughts and ideas, experience and reflection. Questions are asked. Answers are sought. Who am I? Why is the world as it is? Why do people die? Why isn't everybody happy? What is God like? Does God really exist? The world's religions and their founders have asked these questions and given their own very different and yet at the same time very similar answers. "Know yourself." "Know God." These two precepts sum up the religious search and at the same time help us to find again the peace and happiness we knew as children.

The religious quest

T HE WORLD CAN BE an uncomfortable place to live in as well as a cause for excitement and wonder. Life itself can be both puzzling and exhilarating. A person may feel very much alone although surrounded by others. To a great extent, existence and the universe remain a mystery. From the earliest times humankind has set out on a religious quest or spiritual search so that life and death may take on some meaning and significance. Out of this search the world's religions have emerged. Broadly speaking, there are two main traditions. One accepts the essential goodness of the physical world but tries to change the parts of it that seem wrong or broken. The other says that reality is essentially spiritual and seeks to release the soul from an endless round of birth, death, and rebirth in the material world. Religions have several different dimensions. They teach people how to live. They tell myths – stories about the gods and creation, which help to explain life. They offer their followers systems of ideas and beliefs, rituals (set patterns) of worship, social organizations to belong to, and the experience of a greater reality beyond the self.

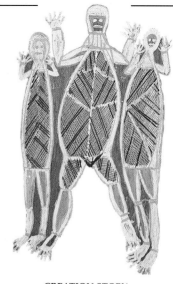

CREATION STORY
This Australian bark painting shows an Aboriginal ancestral group from the Dreamtime, a time when the landscape received its present form. In many religions, moral laws are rooted in beliefs about the creation, or beliefs about ancestors.

LIGHT OF LIFE
Since ancient times, people have recognized that life on Earth depends on the Sun. Many have visualized God as light and life, and have used the Sun as a symbol for God.

Religion is not alien to us....
It is always within us:
with some, consciously;
with others, unconsciously.
But it is always there.

MAHATMA GANDHI

Uluru (previously known as Ayers Rock)

REACHING UPWARD
The seven terraces of the great Buddhist monument of Borobudur in Indonesia are lined with scenes of the Buddha's spiritual progress, carved in stone. As pilgrims walk around and upward, they learn about how to follow his example. At the top is an empty bell-shaped dome, perhaps inviting the presence of the Buddha and his wisdom. Many religions use architecture, sculpture, and the other arts to convey their ideas.

LIFE AND DEATH

Death comes to everyone. It is both welcomed and feared. Yet many people see indications that death is not the end and this life is not the only one. In dreams, people may look at themselves from outside their own bodies. When visiting a new place, they feel sure that they have been there before. They imagine another life where wrongs will be righted. Some believe that the soul is endlessly reborn in different bodies; others, that soul and body are reunited after death. Tombs and funeral rituals may be seen as part of the preparation for the next life.

CLEANSING AND HEALING

Water is essential to life, so springs and rivers have long featured in religion as symbols of spiritual life and centers of pilgrimage. Here, in the Ganges River, India, people drink the holy water or bathe in it for healing and cleansing.

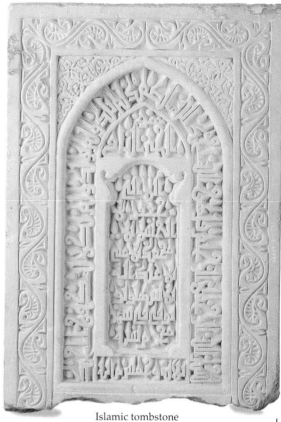

Islamic tombstone

The rock is 1,143 ft (348 m) high, 4 miles (6 km) long, and 1.5 miles (2 km) wide

You have made us for Yourself, and our hearts are restless until they rest in You.

SAINT AUGUSTINE OF HIPPO

HOLY MOUNTAIN

The vast stone outcrop called Uluru, in Australia, is of great spiritual significance to its Aboriginal custodians. Close relationships with the Earth and nature are at the heart of all Aboriginal beliefs and customs. The landscape itself is seen as full of spiritual meaning. Several other religions include similar beliefs, and a number of mountains around the world are considered holy. Some are seen as places where gods live.

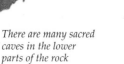

There are many sacred caves in the lower parts of the rock

The Willendorf Venus, an Earth Goddess figure

FERTILITY AND THE MOTHER GODDESS

Life depends on the fertility of the Earth, together with light and water from Heaven. Sun God and Earth Goddess have often been pictured as coming together to produce life. Lesser gods, like Thunder and Rain, and human workers make sure the land is fertile. It is likely that worship of a "Mother Goddess" – associated with springtime and harvest, sowing and reaping, and the bearing of children – is an early, if not the earliest, religious rite.

Life and death in Egypt

THE ANCIENT EGYPTIANS had many gods. The chief of them all was the sun god, who was worshiped in many different forms and seen as responsible for all creation. The other gods each had charge of a different area of life. Believing that all events were controlled by the gods, Egyptians made many offerings to try to keep them happy, hoping that the gods would bless them. And they tried to lead good lives so as to be ready for the judgment of the god Osiris, who ruled the heavenly kingdom in which Egyptians wished to live after death. They pictured this kingdom as a perfect version of Egypt, called the "Field of Reeds." To get there, the dead had to make a difficult journey through the underworld, Duat. If they managed to pass Duat's monsters and lakes of fire, they faced judgment by Osiris in the Hall of Two Truths.

SIGN OF LIFE
Only gods, kings, and queens were allowed to carry the ankh, the sign of life. It showed that they had the power to give life or take it away.

EYE OF HORUS
Wadjet eye amulets were placed on mummies to protect them. A wadjet eye represented the eye the sky god Horus lost fighting the evil Seth, god of chaos and disorder, for the throne of Egypt. Magically restored, it acquired healing properties and symbolized the victory of good over evil. It was said to protect anything behind it.

Outer coffin of Pasenhor, one of many Libyans who settled in Egypt

Symbols were painted on mummy cases to help on the voyage to the afterlife

A HOME FOR THE SPIRIT
The Egyptians prepared for the afterlife in several ways. They mummified the bodies of the dead to make them last forever, so that a dead person's spirit would always have a home. They also filled their tombs with magical protection to help them survive the dangerous journey across Duat, and with food and equipment they might need.

THE PLACE OF JUDGMENT
If the dead managed to cross Duat, they had to pass a final test, set in the Hall of Two Truths. The dead person's heart was weighed in the balance against the Feather of Truth, symbol of Ma'at, goddess of order, truth, and justice, to see if it was heavy with sin. In this picture, the person passes the test and is presented to Osiris. Had he failed, his heart would have been eaten by the monster Ammit.

The dead person is led by the jackal-headed god Anubis

The god Thoth records the result

Ammit, devourer of the dead

The Feather of Truth

The dead person's heart is on one scale

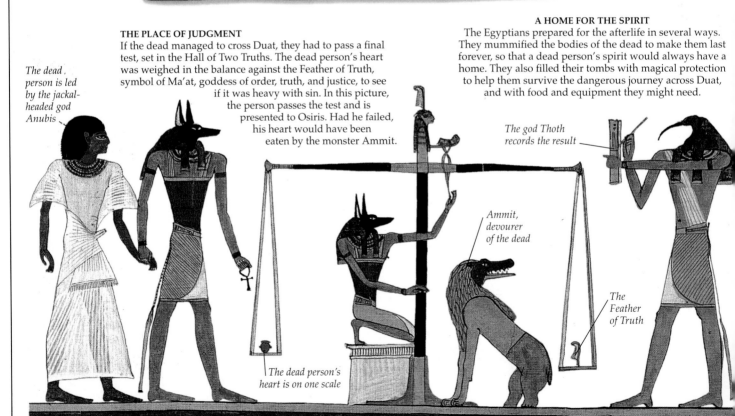

REBIRTH

Many religions have a belief in rebirth, also called new birth or second birth. This can mean passing from childhood to adulthood, awakening to spiritual life, or moving from death to life. It is often symbolized by passing through water or, as in Egypt, by leaving the grave and meeting the god of rebirth.

MAGIC SPELLS

The *Book of the Dead* is a scroll (roll) of papyrus containing a collection of magic spells. Each spell was meant as a prayer or plea from the dead person to help on the voyage through Duat to the heavenly afterlife. This statue of Osiris has a hidden compartment where the scroll was kept.

Roll of papyrus

Secret compartment

Shabti figures

O you living upon earth, who love life and hate death...

INSCRIPTION ON EGYPTIAN TOMB

Box containing the shabti figures shows gods and a priestess

GOD OF REBIRTH

Osiris, god of rebirth, judged people's souls in the afterlife. He was believed to have triumphed over death, and every Egyptian wanted to follow his example. This statue of him would have been placed in a tomb or temple.

Osiris presides over judgment

The guardian goddesses Isis, wife of Osiris, and her sister Nephthys

WORKER FIGURES

The Egyptians believed that after death Osiris might order them to work in the fields in his heavenly land. Rich people provided their mummies with shabtis, carved figures who would spring to life and do their work for them in the afterlife.

The four sons of Horus, guardians of the vital organs, standing on a lotus flower

Gods and nature in Greece

In ANCIENT GREECE, nature was seen to hold the power of life and was therefore sacred. A mountain was the sky god's throne; the god's worshipers did not climb it to admire the view but in order to pray for rain. Every tree had its own spirit; the oak was sacred to Zeus, the olive to Athena, the laurel to Apollo, and the myrtle to Aphrodite. Groves were considered especially holy and were used as places of refuge. Each river also had its god, each spring its nymph, and the sea was home to many deities and spirits. Every area of life was overseen by a deity. The gods intervened in human life as and when they chose, helping those they liked, harming others. Each person could choose his or her own god.

THE PARTHENON
Built between 447 and 432 B.C.E. by the city's leader, Pericles, the Parthenon stood on the highest point of the Acropolis in Athens. It was dedicated to the goddess Athena and housed a huge gold and ivory statue of her.

HUNTER AND MOTHER
Artemis was goddess of hunting and the moon. At Ephesus, Artemis worship merged with that of the Great Mother, an ancient goddess linked with the earth and fertility.

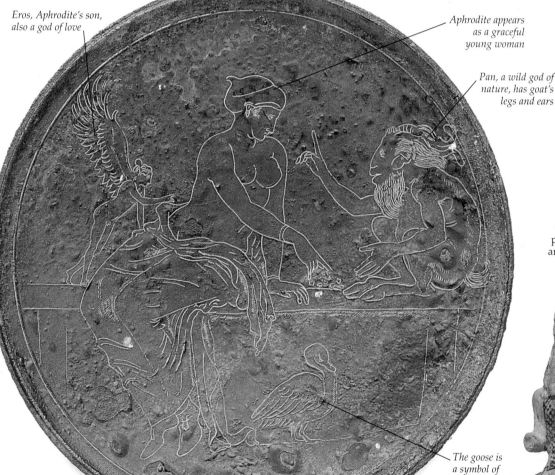

Eros, Aphrodite's son, also a god of love

Aphrodite appears as a graceful young woman

Pan, a wild god of nature, has goat's legs and ears

The goose is a symbol of Aphrodite

APOLLO
Apollo, brother of Artemis, was the model of youthful strength and beauty. A powerful god, he was associated with the Sun, light, prophecy, and healing, but if he was angry, his arrows could cause plague.

GODDESS OF LOVE
Aphrodite was the goddess of love and beauty. She was also called the "foam-born" because she was said to have risen from the sea when it was sprinkled with the seed and blood of ancient, defeated gods. On this mirror case she is playing the ancient game of knucklebones with the goatlike Pan, god of the countryside.

EARTH MOTHER
Demeter was goddess of the harvest. It was said that when her daughter Persephone was stolen by Pluto, ruler of Hades (the underworld), her sorrow made the crops stop growing. Persephone was released, on condition that she had not eaten in Hades. In fact, she had eaten six pomegranate seeds, so had to stay in Hades for six months each year. This story explained why we have seasons.

Demeter and Persephone sit side by side in this terra-cotta figure, probably holding the reins of an ox-cart

Zeus, king of
the gods

*In all things of nature
there is something of
the marvelous.*

ARISTOTLE

Aegeus,
legendary
king of
Athens,
consulting
the oracle

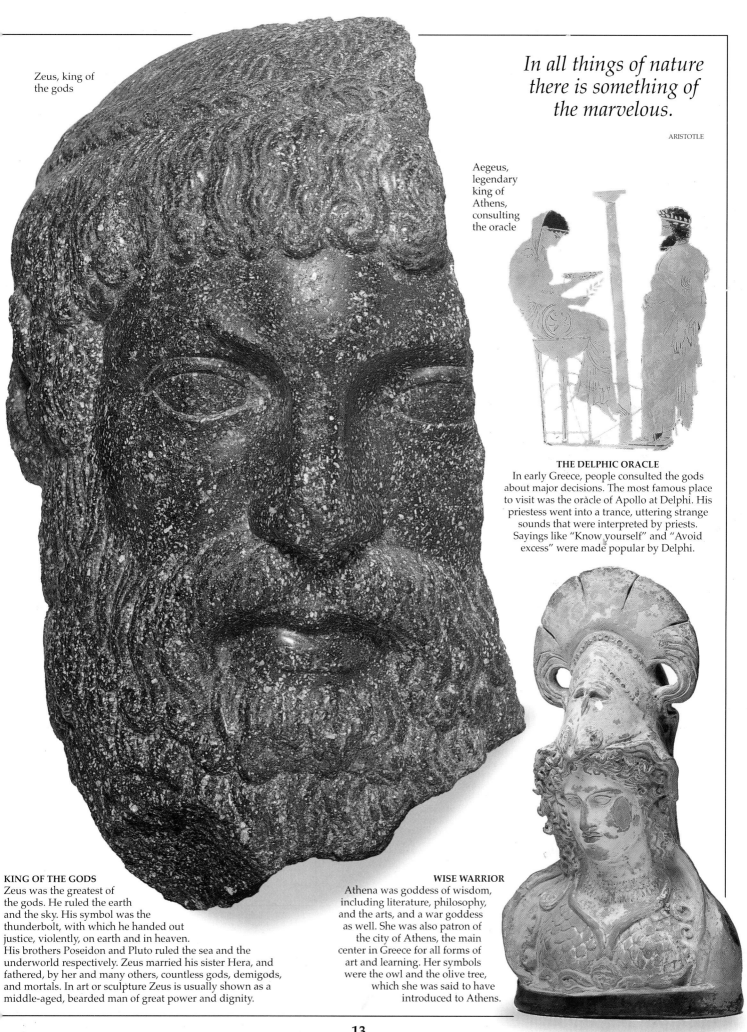

THE DELPHIC ORACLE
In early Greece, people consulted the gods
about major decisions. The most famous place
to visit was the oràcle of Apollo at Delphi. His
priestess went into a trance, uttering strange
sounds that were interpreted by priests.
Sayings like "Know yourself" and "Avoid
excess" were made popular by Delphi.

KING OF THE GODS
Zeus was the greatest of
the gods. He ruled the earth
and the sky. His symbol was the
thunderbolt, with which he handed out
justice, violently, on earth and in heaven.
His brothers Poseidon and Pluto ruled the sea and the
underworld respectively. Zeus married his sister Hera, and
fathered, by her and many others, countless gods, demigods,
and mortals. In art or sculpture Zeus is usually shown as a
middle-aged, bearded man of great power and dignity.

WISE WARRIOR
Athena was goddess of wisdom,
including literature, philosophy,
and the arts, and a war goddess
as well. She was also patron of
the city of Athens, the main
center in Greece for all forms of
art and learning. Her symbols
were the owl and the olive tree,
which she was said to have
introduced to Athens.

The primal vision

THE POWER OF LIFE
There is a widespread belief among primal peoples that all living things are invested with mana (power). Throughout the Pacific islands of Polynesia, the arts, especially wood carving, were used to represent gods, nature spirits, and the spirits of ancestors, and to provide "vehicles" (material "homes") for their mana. This carving, from the Cook Islands, is of a god associated with canoe-making and with bringing good luck to fishermen. The same gods are found again and again among the many different peoples of Polynesia, sometimes under different names.

Iɴ ᴀғʀɪᴄᴀ, ᴛʜᴇ ᴀᴍᴇʀɪᴄᴀs, and Oceania, perhaps 250 million people live in "primal" or "traditional" societies. For them, all of life is religious; nothing that they think or say or do takes place outside a spiritual framework, and they look to the spiritual world for help and blessing. Those who live along Africa's Rift Valley, on the plains of the Americas, or on Pacific islands, associate God with the sun and sky, and they organize their lesser gods to mirror their own societies. The Masai of East Africa worship One God linked with the sun, while the Yoruba people of Nigeria worship a High God who rules over many lesser gods. People living in rainforests, or in densely settled areas, worship the spirits or powers of nature and venerate (give great respect and honor to) their ancestors. Rituals to do with the spirits and powers are often complex; those to do with the High God tend to be simpler.

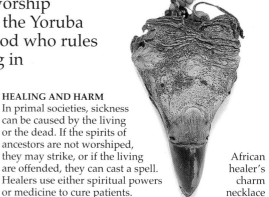

HEALING AND HARM
In primal societies, sickness can be caused by the living or the dead. If the spirits of ancestors are not worshiped, they may strike, or if the living are offended, they can cast a spell. Healers use either spiritual powers or medicine to cure patients.

African healer's charm necklace

SACRIFICE

From the earliest times, sacrifice has been offered to ancestors, spirits, or gods to avert their anger or express thanks or for other reasons. It has often required the laying down of life, usually of animals such as cattle and sheep. Sometimes worshipers sacrifice by giving up pleasures or possessions.

Doll made from stick, beeswax, beads, hide

Two fertility dolls from Angola in Southwest Africa (center and right)

Central part of doll made from corn cob

Fertility doll from Cameroon in West Africa

OSHUN SHRINE
Among the Yoruba, the major goddess is Oshun, the river goddess. It is said that the work of the male gods was failing until she joined them. Women who wish to become pregnant and persons who desire protection from disease appeal to Oshun.

FERTILE EARTH
Many primal peoples look to the spirits and ancestors to give them the sun, rain, and fertile earth that they need. They also need large families, and pray to spirits, ancestors, and Mother Earth to make the women fertile. In some societies girls and young women carry fertility dolls such as these to make them fertile.

The metal acts like a mirror to reflect any evil that threatens the ancestor

Each of the three main figures carries signs of leadership: knife, tusk, and elaborate headdress

These heads may represent family slaves

Kota guardian figure made of wood covered in brass

GUARDIAN FIGURE
Some societies believe that the physical remains of important people can hold something of the power those people had in their lifetimes. Among the Kota people of Gabon, the skulls and bones of important ancestors are kept in baskets in a special hut and offerings are made to them. Guardian figures such as this are placed on such baskets to protect the ancestors' remains from evil forces.

Those who are dead are never gone.

AFRICAN PROVERB

The three figures would originally have worn cloth wraps over their legs

ANCESTRAL SCREEN
It is believed that ancestors will protect and guide living relatives who honor them. Among the Kalabari people of Nigeria, screens such as this one were placed behind altars, where descendants made offerings to the spirit of the ancestor depicted on the screen. On this screen, the central figure is the head of a prosperous trading house. He is standing with two sons or attendants.

Rituals of life

Sande initiation mask

RITUALS OF LIFE play a major role in primal societies. They are largely of two kinds: "rites of passage" and "rites of affliction." Rites of passage take place at important moments of a person's journey through life, such as birth, puberty, marriage, divorce, and death. Rites of affliction arise at times of crisis such as illness or disaster. The rituals are usually divided into three stages: separation from the old, transition, and inclusion into the new. For example, young people at puberty may be separated from society (and, symbolically, from childhood), then instructed on how to be adults, and then incorporated back into society as full adult members of their communities. In some societies the rituals may be performed by priests, in others by ritual leaders, or shamans, or healers.

FUNERAL DANCE
Funeral rites are important in primal religions. Among the Dogon people of West Africa, they are occasions for elaborate public dances (above) accompanied by chants in a secret language. The rite retells the Dogon myth of how death entered the world – through the disobedience of young men. The Awa masked society also helps to preserve other popular Dogon myths. Here the dancers are wearing skirts dyed in red, the color associated with death.

ELEPHANT SPIRIT MASK
Many African peoples make masks, mainly to represent the spirits who are called on to be present at various ceremonies. Some spirit masks have human features, others have those of animals. The masks are not made to look realistic. Instead, traditional symbolic styles are followed; they are understood by ritual experts who interpret for the people. This elephant spirit mask was made by an Ibo artist of Nigeria. The elephant spirit is a symbol of ugliness.

This mask is worn on top of the head

INITIATION MASK
Among the Mende people of West Africa, girls are initiated at puberty into the Sande Society, a women's secret association. Elders instruct them in domestic and craft skills and prepare them for marriage and motherhood. As part of the initiation a masked dance, or masquerade, is held. This gives people a chance to express themselves through a ceremony that unites them. Sande masks represent power, emotion, and womanly qualities. They symbolically express the Mende ideal of female beauty.

The use of cowrie shells in decoration is widespread and usually symbolizes fertility

There is no distinction between religion and the rest of life. All of life is religious.

AFRICAN SAYING

INITIATION MASK
Masks can represent important ancestors. This royal initiation mask comes from the Kuba kingdom in Zaire. It represents the son of the first divine king. Masks play an important role in initiation ceremonies. Other Kuba masks, made to look like spirits, were worn by chiefs to enforce discipline.

SPIRITS AND HEALING
In primal societies all forces that affect people, good or bad, are seen as coming from the spirits. For example, there are spirits of technology, such as the motor car, and spirits of illnesses. Sometimes these spirits, such as the Yoruba smallpox spirit above, are represented by images and are invoked, or called on, for healing and blessing.

SUMMONING THE SPIRITS
Among the original peoples of the far north of North America and Asia, those who get in touch with the spirit world are known as shamans. Shamans' masks, such as this Alaskan one, are worn at various festivals and at rituals of healing and of divination (seeing into the future).

Four oval faces, each flanked by a pair of upraised hands, surround the central face of the Sun

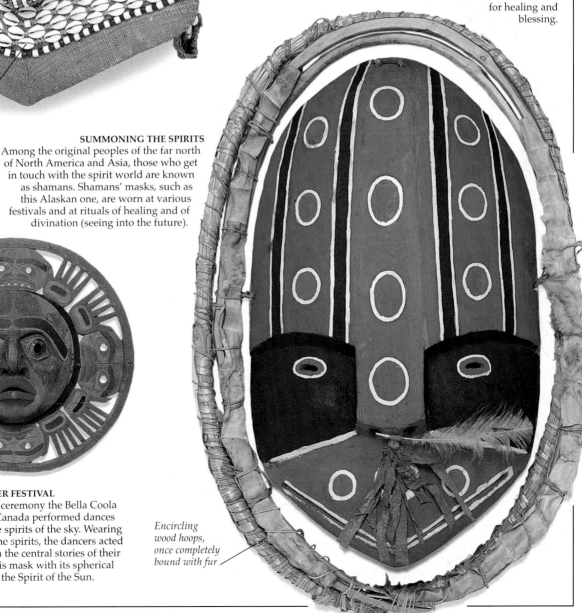

WINTER FESTIVAL
During their winter ceremony the Bella Coola people of western Canada performed dances taught to them by the spirits of the sky. Wearing masks representing the spirits, the dancers acted out with great drama the central stories of their people's beliefs. This mask with its spherical face represents the Spirit of the Sun.

Encircling wood hoops, once completely bound with fur

The Hindu way

SACRED SOUND
Om or Aum is the eternal syllable. It is said or sung before and after all prayers.

To BE A HINDU is to be born a Hindu and then to follow a certain way of life. The word "Hindu" comes from Hind, the old Persian word for India, and Hinduism simply means the religion of the peoples of India. With no founder and no creed, it has evolved over time. As we know it today, it can be compared to a great, deep river into which, over a period of more than 3,000 years, many streams have flowed. The streams are the beliefs and practices of the numerous races, ethnic groups, and cultures of the Indian subcontinent. Hinduism has many gods, yet, for some Hindus, there is an impersonal "Absolute" behind them all, called Brahman, creator of the universe. Brahman "unfolds" into the Trimurti, the holy trinity made up of Brahma, Vishnu, and Shiva. Brahma is the creator; Vishnu, the great preserver; and Shiva, the destroyer but also the re-creator. Hindus everywhere believe in reincarnation, that the individual soul is born again in another body and that life flows on through many existences, from birth through death to rebirth. If people are good in one life, they will be rewarded by being well born in their next life.

Brahma has four heads; this sculpture shows three of them

BRAHMA THE CREATOR
Brahma's exclusive purpose is creation. Unlike Vishnu and Shiva, he does not contain opposites within himself, and so he never destroys what he has created. According to one tradition, he arose out of the "egg of the universe." Originally he had only one head. He acquired three more when he created woman. After cutting her from his own body he fell in love with her, but she hid herself from him. So that he could always see her from every side, he grew heads to the right, left, and behind.

VISHNU THE PRESERVER
Vishnu contains and balances good and evil, and all other opposites, within himself. His main task, as preserver, is to maintain the divine order of the universe, keeping the balance between good and evil powers. When evil gets the upper hand, Vishnu comes down to Earth to restore the balance, taking the form of one of ten incarnations called avataras – beings in whom he lives throughout their lives. Two of the best known avataras are Krishna and Rama. Vishnu is often called "the infinite ocean of the universe."

Smaller figures represent two of the four Vedas (earliest holy scriptures)

HINDUISM

ONE GOD?	Yes, Brahman who appears in unlimited forms. Each Hindu worships one of these many forms, e.g., Brahma, Vishnu, Shiva, Sarasvati, Kali, Lakshmi…
THE AFTERLIFE?	Reincarnation
SCRIPTURES?	*Vedas, Upanishads,* and others
MAJOR FESTIVALS?	Divali – New year Festival of Lights Holi – Spring festival Janmashtami – Birthday of Krishna Shivaratri – Main festival of Shiva
SACRED ANIMAL?	Cow is the symbol of Earth

Hinduism is more a way of life than a set of beliefs.

SARVEPALLI RADHAKRISHNAN
FORMER PRESIDENT OF INDIA

The flaming halo around Shiva symbolizes the cosmos

Shiva's whirling hair holds flowers, snakes, a skull, and a small figure of the goddess Ganga (the sacred river Ganges)

As Shiva beats the drum, he summons up a new creation

Shiva's vertical third eye gives light to the world

The flame is a symbol of the fire with which Shiva destroys the universe

This hand points to the left foot, beneath which the worshiper can find safe refuge

SHIVA AS "LORD OF THE DANCE"
Shiva is both destroyer and re-creator. He is depicted in many forms. As Nataraja, Lord of the Dance (the form shown here), he brings the dance or cycle of life to an end in order that a new cycle of life may begin. This statue illustrates a legend in which he subdued 10,000 heretics (nonbelievers) by dancing on the demon of ignorance.

Left foot is a symbol of liberation

Apasmarapurusa, the Black Dwarf, demon of ignorance

Shiva dances in a ring of flames

Shiva is adored by two sages (wise men); the one on his right has the lower body of a snake, the one on his left has tiger legs

This sage has the legs of a tiger

Flowers, symbols of purity, and rebirth, are used to decorate temples and statues

Gods and heroes

THE HINDU SCRIPTURES are full of the adventures of numerous gods and heroes. The *Vedas* tell of Agni the god of fire and sacrifice, Indra the sky-god of war, and Varuna the god of cosmic order. The two great Hindu epics, the *Ramayana* and *Mahabharata*, weave their tales around Rama and Krishna, the most popular of the ten avatars (incarnations or forms) of Vishnu. Within the *Mahabharata* is the frequently translated great Indian spiritual classic, *Bhagavad Gita*, the "Song of the Lord." This poem takes the form of a dialogue between the warrior Arjuna and Krishna, his charioteer, as together they fight the war between good and evil symbolized in the battle between the closely related families of the Pandavas and the Kauravas.

Matsya, the fish and first avatara, warned humanity of a great flood

Narasimha, the man-lion and fourth avatara, defeated demons

Kalki, the tenth avatara, is still to come

PRAYING IN THE GANGES
The river Ganges is a sacred river to Hindus, a symbol of life without end. Pilgrims from all over India come to bathe in its holy waters. Varanasi (Benares) on the Ganges is India's most sacred city and the desired place of death for every Hindu.

Krishna's skin is blue, the color of the oceans and the sky

The flute is a symbol of the cowherds with whom Krishna spent his early years

Krishna is standing on a lotus flower, a symbol of purity and fertility

KRISHNA AVATARA
Many colorful stories are woven around Krishna, eighth avatara of Vishnu. They are told in the great epic, the *Mahabharata*. Vishnu was persuaded to come down to Earth as Krishna when demons were about to overcome the gods. On hearing the news of Krishna's arrival, the demon-king Kansa planned to kill him. But Krishna was fostered by a poor woman called Yashoda, who kept him safe. Countless tales are told of his childish pranks, youthful adventures, and later battles with the demons.

In this ivory image Durga kills the buffalo demon Mahisha

In each of her ten hands Durga holds a special weapon; each weapon is a symbol of divine power

THE GODDESS DURGA
Durga (also known as Parvati and Kali) is one of the many forms assumed by Mahadevi Shakti, Shiva's consort. She is the warrior who fights the demons that represent the lowest human passions. The worship of Durga often provides the opportunity for some of the greatest Hindu festivals.

In this picture, Rama and Sita sit together, with Rama's faithful brother Laksmana behind them

Hanuman, the monkey god, loyal ally of Rama

RAMA AVATARA

Rama, seventh avatara of Vishnu, is the embodiment of goodness come down to Earth. He and his wife, Sita, are models of loving husband and faithful wife. He is respected as the virtuous god-king who overthrew the wicked demon Ravana. First, he and Sita were banished, then Ravana kidnapped Sita. But Rama defeated Ravana with the help of Hanuman, the brave monkey god, and his monkey army.

I am the beginning and the middle and the end of all that is. Of all knowledge I am the knowledge of the Soul.

KRISHNA IN *BHAGAVAD GITA* 10:32

Ganesha's half-halo indicates his divinity

The crown shows kingly status

Noose to snare delusion

This decorated goad (pointed stick) represents self-control

The large flapping ears separate the essential from the nonessential

Ganesha writes with a piece of his broken tusk after his steel pen snapped

Modaka sweets

GANESHA

Ganesha is the first-born son of Shiva and his beautiful wife Parvati. It is told how Shiva, returning after a long absence to his heavenly dwelling, saw a stranger at his door and promptly cut off his head. Parvati appeared, only to find that the victim was their own son. Desperate to make amends, Shiva cut off the head of a passing elephant and placed it on his son's shoulders. From that day on, Ganesha has had an elephant's head. He is the god of wisdom and the remover of obstacles. In their prayers, Hindus ask him to take note of their requests and convey them to Shiva.

Ganesha's great belly represents space, big enough to hold all wisdom and life

Three ways to salvation

HINDUS WISH TO ACHIEVE SALVATION, or moksha, by release from the cycle of rebirth. Lightening the load of bad karma – guilt acquired through wrong living – leads toward the final release. There are three basic ways of achieving salvation. The way of action involves performing correct religious observances, in the hope of being blessed by the divine for fulfilling these duties. The way of knowledge seeks to understand and experience the ultimate meaning of life through reason and meditation, as sadhus do. The way of devotion (the most popular way) seeks to be united with the divine through the worship of a particular deity. Traditionally, Hindus are born into one of four castes (social classes), or are "untouchables" (outcastes – the lowest rank). Religious duties vary with caste.

HOLY MAN
A sadhu is a wandering holy man. He has no possessions apart from his robes and a few utensils.

WEDDING
Hindu families go to great expense to provide a wedding ceremony for their children. Marriages are arranged according to caste, kinship, and horoscope. The wedding ceremony contains many highly symbolic elements, and the institution of marriage is highly valued.

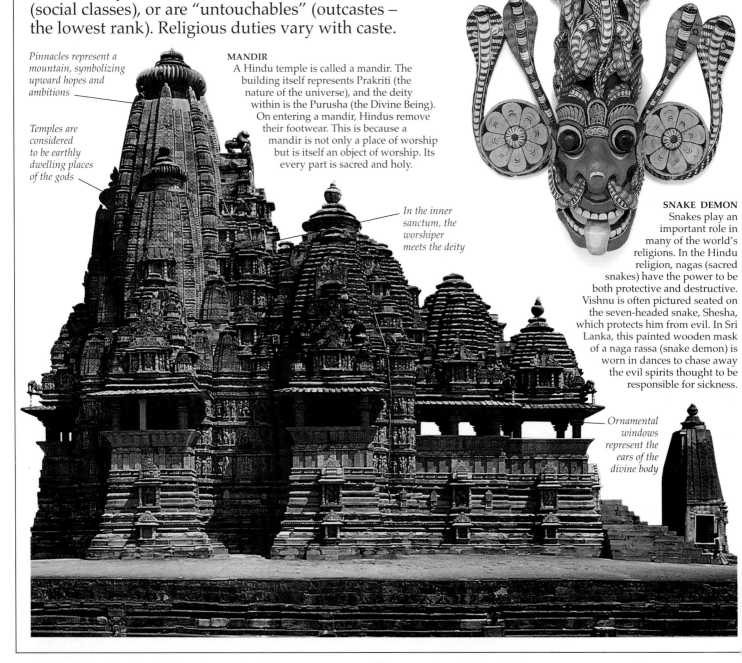

Pinnacles represent a mountain, symbolizing upward hopes and ambitions

MANDIR
A Hindu temple is called a mandir. The building itself represents Prakriti (the nature of the universe), and the deity within is the Purusha (the Divine Being). On entering a mandir, Hindus remove their footwear. This is because a mandir is not only a place of worship but is itself an object of worship. Its every part is sacred and holy.

Temples are considered to be earthly dwelling places of the gods

In the inner sanctum, the worshiper meets the deity

SNAKE DEMON
Snakes play an important role in many of the world's religions. In the Hindu religion, nagas (sacred snakes) have the power to be both protective and destructive. Vishnu is often pictured seated on the seven-headed snake, Shesha, which protects him from evil. In Sri Lanka, this painted wooden mask of a naga rassa (snake demon) is worn in dances to chase away the evil spirits thought to be responsible for sickness.

Ornamental windows represent the ears of the divine body

INCARNATION

The idea that God or the gods can appear in bodily form, usually human, is found in many religions. In Hinduism, Vishnu comes down to Earth a number of times in different forms known as avataras. In Christianity, God makes Himself manifest in Jesus Christ.

Incense holder

The lotus, a symbol of purity, fertility, and creation, is linked with Vishnu

Kemal (lotus-shaped scent shaker) used in domestic worship

Main image of Vishnu

Krishna and Balarama

DAILY WORSHIP
Hindus perform puja (daily rites of worship), not only in the temple but also in the home. Many families set aside a room for worship; others erect a shrine or image, or display a holy picture, in one corner. This is a portable shrine of Vishnu and shows Vishnu under the protection of Shesha (the serpent), with Krishna avatara and his half-brother Balarama.

INCENSE
Incense is made from a number of woods and resins that, when heated or burned, give off a fragrant aroma. The use of incense in divine worship is an ancient and widespread practice. It is associated with sacrifice, honor, purification, and celebration.

Give me your mind and give me your heart, give me your offerings and your adoration.

KRISHNA IN *BHAGAVAD GITA 9.34*

The warrior Arjuna

Krishna, acting as Arjuna's charioteer

CHARIOT AND CHARIOTEER
In the *Bhagavad Gita* there is a dialogue between the god Krishna and the archer Arjuna on a battlefield. The battle is the war between good and evil, action and inaction, knowledge and ignorance, belief and disbelief. Krishna urges Arjuna to action and promises to be his charioteer. Vivekananda, a modern reformer and philosopher, interpreted their relationship: The body is the chariot; the outer senses are the horses; the mind the reins; and the intellect the charioteer. So man crosses the ocean of maya (illusion). He goes beyond and reaches God. When a man is under the control of his senses, he is of this world. When he has controlled the senses, he has renounced the world.

This picture shows a famous scene from the *Bhagavad Gita*

23

The Buddhist path

SIDDHARTHA GAUTAMA, THE FOUNDER of Buddhism, lived in the 6th century B.C.E. in northern India. He was brought up to become a king and married a beautiful princess who bore him a son. As a young prince, his father protected him from all the sadness of the world outside his palaces. However, while his son was still young, Gautama managed to slip out, and encountered the "Four Sights." First was an old man, second a man sick with disease, and third a corpse being carried to the cremation ground. Finally, he saw a religious beggar with a shaved head, wearing a simple yellow robe but radiating peace and joy. It was then that Gautama made his "Great Renunciation," leaving his family and life of great comfort to find the answers to this suffering he had seen. For six years he tried and failed, until he went to meditate under a bodhi (or bo) tree, where he received his "Great Enlightenment" and became Buddha, which means "Enlightened One."

THE NOBLE EIGHTFOLD PATH
The eight-spoked wheel is a symbol of the Eightfold Path, which is a summary of the Buddha's teaching about how to escape suffering and find enlightenment. The eight stages to follow were: right thought, right understanding, right speech, right action, right livelihood, right effort, right concentration, and right contemplation.

Eyes cast down to show he is meditating; face calm and peaceful

RENUNCIATION
Gautama's decision to leave his family is known as the Great Renunciation. For the next six years, he tried to find release from the weariness of existence. He was reduced to skin and bones but could not reach this goal. So he left his companions and went to meditate under a bodhi tree near the river Ganges.

Right hand points down, asking the Earth to witness his enlightenment

The Buddha, meditating: in meditation Buddhists seek to empty their minds of all distracting thoughts and to gain perfect peace.

Buddha's cross-legged position is called the lotus position

Halo, one of the marks of Buddhahood

ENLIGHTENMENT
While meditating under the bodhi tree, Gautama learned "the Four Noble Truths": that all life is suffering; that the cause of suffering is desire; that the end of desire means the end of suffering; that desire can be stopped by following the Eightfold Path. The Eightfold Path is also called the Middle Way because it avoids both living for pleasure and too much self-denial.

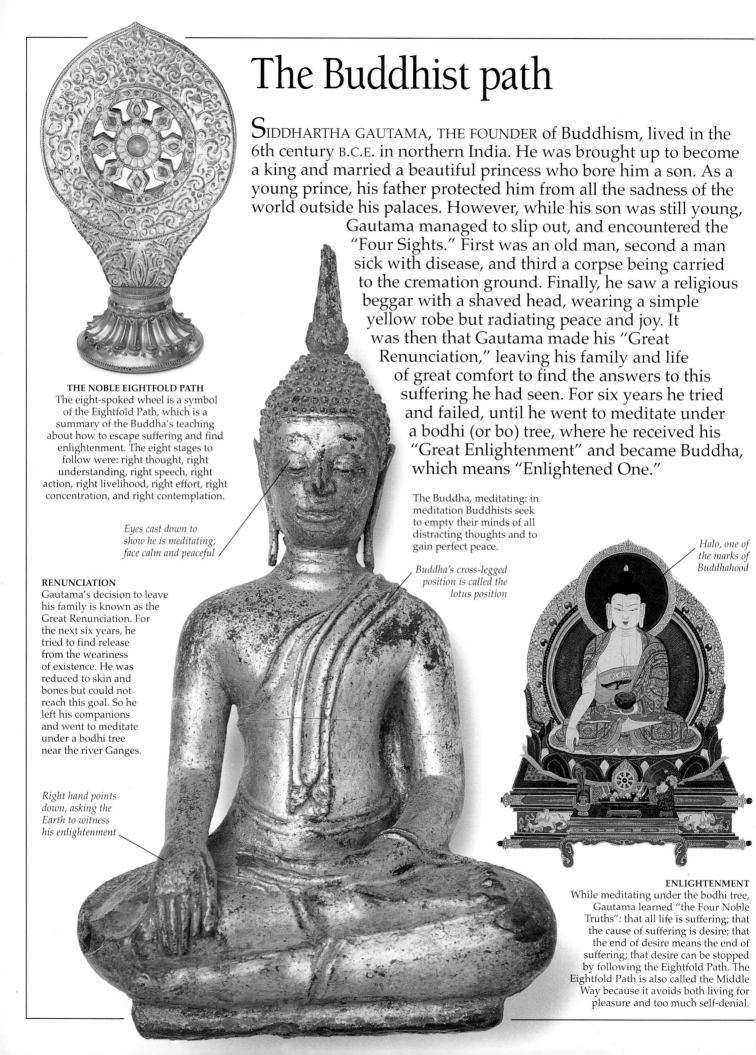

Cultivating enlightenment with the pure mind of meditation… you will completely pass beyond the suffering of this world.

GAUTAMA BUDDHA

BUDDHA IMAGES
Here, a Buddhist monk kneels in prayer before a large Buddha image. As Buddhism spread from north India across Asia, the Buddha came to be venerated rather like a god. More and more images of him were made.

The Lord of Death holds the wheel to symbolize the limits of life

The Wheel of Life, or the Everlasting Round

Pictures in outer circle teach about karma

Pictures in inner circle show the six realms (states) of existence

The pig, cock, and snake represent the poisons of greed, delusion, and hatred, the three ingredients of ignorance that underlie all forms of suffering

The Realm of Humans: full of selfishness, ignorance, and desire, but there is also the path to enlightenment

The Realm of Beasts, ruled by ignorance, apathy, and instinct

The realm of the Denizens of Hell, full of hatred and anger; a Buddha preaches patience and hope

The Realm of the Gods, happy and proud

The Realm of the Titans, in which demi-gods fight endlessly, motivated by envy

The Realm of the Hungry Spirits: consumed by greed, they suffer permanent hunger and thirst

In each realm a Buddha-figure appears and helps the beings there

WHEEL OF EXISTENCE
According to the Buddha's teaching, when people die, they are reborn into one of the six realms of existence. Which realm depends on how they behaved in their previous life. This is called karma: the law by which actions are rewarded or punished as they deserve, the law of cause and effect in moral life. Your karma determines whether your next life will be better or worse than this one. The aim of Gautama's search was to escape this cycle of rebirth, to find the state of happiness known as Nirvana.

Devotion and meditation

As BUDDHISM SPREAD OUTWARD from India, it developed into two different branches. They are often called "vehicles" since Buddhist Dharma (teaching or law) is thought of as a raft or ship carrying people across an ocean of suffering to Nirvana – a "Beyond" of salvation and bliss. Theravada, the "Little Vehicle," is mainly found in Southeast Asia. It emphasizes the life of meditation lived by the monk, and its teaching tends towards the view that people are essentially on their own in the universe and can reach Nirvana only by their own efforts. Mahayana, the "Great Vehicle," is dominant in Tibet, China, Korea, Vietnam, and Japan. Mahayana Buddhists believe that people are not alone and must help one another. They can also receive help from the Buddha, other buddhas, and from bodhisattvas (almost-buddhas who have paused before Nirvana to assist others). Salvation is available to all through faith and devotion.

PLACES OF WORSHIP
After the Buddha's death, his body was cremated and his ashes distributed among his followers. They formed the original relics (holy objects) and were housed and worshiped in stupas (great sacred mounds). In parts of Asia stupas are called pagodas. Later, temples were built where worship was offered in the presence of Buddha images and bodhisattvas.

Monks in the precincts of the Wat Po temple in Thailand

PLACES OF MEDITATION
Buddhism gave rise to numerous sects and practices within and outside the two main vehicles. One is Zen, which originated in Chinese ways of meditation. Zen is widespread in Japan, and there are Zen gardens across the country. Zen meditation has strict rules. The most important are to sit in the lotus position and to address riddles that have no answer (these help in breaking free from the mind). For example, "When you clap hands, you hear a sound. Now listen to one hand clapping."

Bodhisattva Avalokiteshvara (which means "The Lord Who Looks Down")

FOCUS OF DEVOTION
Originally the Buddha was a famous and greatly honored human being devoted to working out his own salvation and teaching others. Eventually, in Mahayana Buddhism, he came to be revered as a supernatural being. His image sits in temples. Beside it may be other buddhas, and also bodhisattvas, beings who have reached enlightenment but hold back on the threshold of Nirvana to help others find salvation.

Buddha Amoghasiddhi, one of the five "Meditation Buddhas"

Dipankara Buddha (the "Causer of Light")

Seven other bodhisattvas

Belt or girdle

Razor

Needle and thread

Sharpening stone

Water strainer

Worn around hips

Worn over shoulder

Worn on top for ceremonial occasions or for traveling

To the Buddha for refuge I go,
To the Dharma for refuge I go,
To the Sangha for refuge I go.

GAUTAMA BUDDHA

THAI MONK'S EQUIPMENT

Buddhist monks have very few possessions and live very simple lives. In their daily devotions, both monks and lay people (non-clergy) undertake not to cause injury, steal, consume intoxicating things, engage in wrong sexual behavior, or deceive.

Alms bowl

REINCARNATION

The belief that we live many different lives on earth. When we die we spend time in a disembodied state before being reborn in a different bodily form. What we are reborn as depends on our previous behavior (this is the law of karma). Buddhist and Hindu forms of this belief differ. Buddhists prefer the word rebirth.

Lid from alms bowl used as plate

MONK IN MEDITATION

After his enlightenment, the Buddha formed a community of monks. Ever since, the Sangha, the community of monks, has been central to Buddhism. Even today, in Buddhist Thailand, it is customary for most young men to enter a monastery, if only for a month. Meditation is also very important. In meditation Buddhists attempt to still the mind and its endless flow of thoughts, ideas, and desires, replacing them with a state of inner stillness. In this stillness, it is said, meditators become aware of their fundamental state and gain, in time, enlightenment.

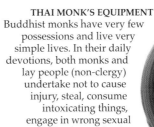

Hands in meditative position

Mat for meditation

Legs crossed in half-lotus position

The Buddhism of Tibet

BUDDHISM CAME TO TIBET from India in the eighth century. By that time Indian Buddhism had adapted a complicated set of rituals and "magic" from folk religion to help people find their way to Nirvana. This form of Buddhism was written in sacred, secret books called tantras, so it was called Tantrism. It included the use of mystic diagrams, called mandalas, and sacred phrases or sayings called mantras, which disciples said over and over again. The religion that came to dominate Tibet was a mixture of Tantric and other Mahayana teachings. In Tibet, it was developed further by spiritual leaders called lamas, who are usually monks. Lamas belong to a number of different groups, or schools. These schools are based around various powerful monasteries. Their ideas and practices vary, but they have usually existed in harmony. One of a lama's tasks is to guide a dying person's spirit in the time between death and rebirth. Lamas spend many years learning and meditating to gain this wisdom.

TIBET AND BEYOND
In modern times Tibetan Buddhism has had an increasing influence abroad. Tibetans and Buddhists of different traditions, such as these monks in Shanghai, are happy to share their experience and wisdom.

Vairochana, foremost of the Meditation Buddhas, perfects knowledge

Amitabha, "Infinite Compassion," perfects speech

Ratnasambhava, "The Beautifier," perfects goodness and beauty

Vajrasattva, "The Unchanging," perfects wisdom

Amoghasiddhi, "Almighty Conqueror," perfects action

THE FIVE BUDDHAS
This Tibetan lama's ritual headdress displays the "Buddhas of Meditation." According to *The Tibetan Book of the Dead*, these buddhas dwell in the heavenly worlds. Each personifies an aspect of "Divine Being," the ultimate reality or wisdom. They meet a dead person's spirit, and the spirit's reaction shows how enlightened the person is and decides how the person will be reborn.

The demon has glaring eyes, protruding tusks, and jutting tongue

RITUAL PROTECTION
In Indian mythology, the god Shiva creates a demon who will be the supreme destructive force of the universe. The grotesque face of this demon, called "the face of glory," is often placed on temples of Shiva as a protective device. This ritual amulet is a Tibetan adaptation of the Indian symbol and is worn to terrify demons and protect the wearer.

VENERATING RELICS

Soon after the Buddha's death, Buddhists began to collect the physical remains and belongings of holy persons and to venerate them as relics. Here, impressions of shrines and Buddha images have been molded from lama ashes. After the cremation of a lama, his ashes are collected, mixed with clay, molded into tablets, and placed in cases or shrines.

Bodhisattvas have graceful bodies, wear long robes and jewelry, and hold religious implements

BODHISATTVA OF COMPASSION

The story is told of how Avalokiteshvara, the Bodhisattva of Compassion, vowed to save all conscious beings, but he soon became so overwhelmed by the task that his head split into a thousand pieces. The pieces were put back together again to form eleven heads, looking in all directions. With these heads and a thousand arms, nowhere is out of reach of his love and mercy. In China he is Kuan Yin and in Japan Kannon, Goddess of Love and Mercy. In Tibet today he becomes reincarnate in the person of the Dalai Lama, now in exile but still the leading lama and Tibet's most important leader.

PRAYER WHEEL

A prayer wheel contains a mantra, a prayer or chant that is repeated many times. Each turn of the wheel counts as a prayer said and merit gained. The mantra in this prayer wheel is usually translated as "Hail to the jewel in the lotus" and is directed to Avalokiteshvara.

Chain helps wheel to spin

Mantra fits inside prayer wheel

He holds objects that illustrate Buddhist truths

As the wheel is spun, the heavy head spins fast

This Avalokiteshvara stands on a lotus-flower throne, which rises on a stalk out of swirling waters

When the breath has ceased… the Knower will be experiencing the Clear Light of the natural condition.

TIBETAN BOOK OF THE DEAD, 1.i

This 18th-century statue is made of gilt bronze

YOUNG LAMAS

Tibetan Buddhism has had a strong spiritual and moral influence on Tibetans. Since the Communist Chinese takeover of 1950, monasteries have been destroyed and the influence of religion weakened. Many do still practice their devotions, however, and a strong movement continues among refugees. Here, young lamas blow horns as part of a monastic ritual.

Confucian piety

CONFUCIUS
Confucius, or K'ung Fu-tzu, (551–479 B.C.E.) was China's first great philosopher. His name means "Master King." A legend says that when he was born, it was foretold that he would be "a king without a crown." His discussions and sayings are collected in *The Analects*.

FOR MANY, CONFUCIANISM is a way of life, a code of behavior, rather than a religion. Confucians may combine following their master, Confucius, with belief in any god, or none. Confucius stressed the importance of *li*, which means proper or orderly conduct. He taught his followers to be "gentlemen." A gentleman is always courteous, fair, respectful to his superiors, and kind to ordinary people. He also practices "filial piety" – his duty to respect and care for his parents. Because of his belief in filial piety, Confucius supported the ancient practice of venerating (giving great respect and honor to) ancestors. He wished to bring order and harmony to society, with everyone doing their duty. He taught that worshiping God and the spirits and honoring one's ancestors means nothing unless service to other people comes first.

THE THREE WAYS
China is the land of the "Three Ways," Confucianism, Taoism, and Buddhism. For more than 2,000 years, they have all played a major role in Chinese life and thought. Confucianism emphasized order and respect, Taoism provided a mystical understanding of the world, and Buddhism offered salvation through compassion and devotion. As they have developed, they have merged with each other, and with the age-old folk religion of China, which is centered on home and family. This painting symbolically shows how the Three Ways mix by placing together their three founders: Buddha (left), Confucius (center), and Lao-tzu (right).

CONFUCIUS DAY CEREMONY
Confucius did not try to found a religion. He just taught a way of life based on rules of good behavior. However, after his death, shrines were built in his honor, and Confucianism became the state religion of China.

Modern Confucian temple at Taipei in Taiwan

Priests honour Confucius Day

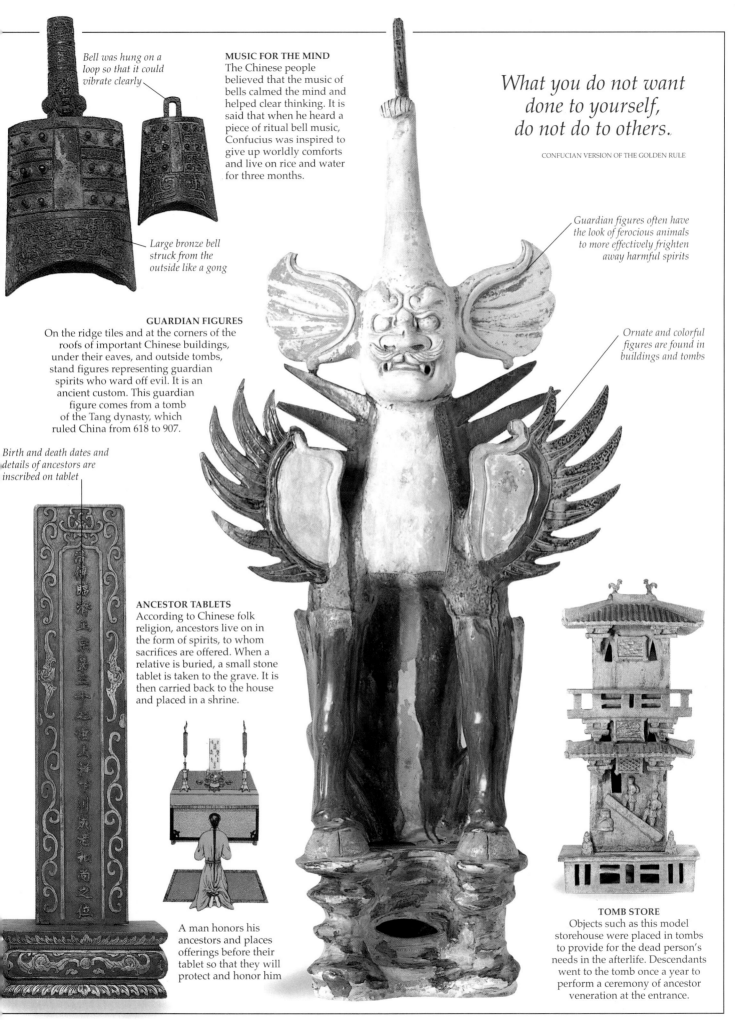

Bell was hung on a loop so that it could vibrate clearly

MUSIC FOR THE MIND
The Chinese people believed that the music of bells calmed the mind and helped clear thinking. It is said that when he heard a piece of ritual bell music, Confucius was inspired to give up worldly comforts and live on rice and water for three months.

Large bronze bell struck from the outside like a gong

What you do not want done to yourself, do not do to others.

CONFUCIAN VERSION OF THE GOLDEN RULE

Guardian figures often have the look of ferocious animals to more effectively frighten away harmful spirits

GUARDIAN FIGURES
On the ridge tiles and at the corners of the roofs of important Chinese buildings, under their eaves, and outside tombs, stand figures representing guardian spirits who ward off evil. It is an ancient custom. This guardian figure comes from a tomb of the Tang dynasty, which ruled China from 618 to 907.

Ornate and colorful figures are found in buildings and tombs

Birth and death dates and details of ancestors are inscribed on tablet

ANCESTOR TABLETS
According to Chinese folk religion, ancestors live on in the form of spirits, to whom sacrifices are offered. When a relative is buried, a small stone tablet is taken to the grave. It is then carried back to the house and placed in a shrine.

A man honors his ancestors and places offerings before their tablet so that they will protect and honor him

TOMB STORE
Objects such as this model storehouse were placed in tombs to provide for the dead person's needs in the afterlife. Descendants went to the tomb once a year to perform a ceremony of ancestor veneration at the entrance.

The Tao principle

TAOISTS BELIEVE THAT THERE IS a principle, or force, running through the whole of the natural world and controlling it. They call this principle the Tao. Tao means way, or path. To follow the Tao is to follow the way of nature. It is sometimes called the "watercourse way" because Taoists see water as a picture of the Tao at work. Water is soft and yielding, it flows effortlessly to humble places, yet it is also the most powerful of substances and nourishes all life. There are two kinds of Taoism: the popular and the philosophical. The followers of philosophical Taoism are likely to be mystical and peaceful. By stilling the inner self, their senses and appetites, they gain an understanding of the Tao and try to live in oneness and harmony with it. The focus of popular Taoism is different. It includes many gods, goddesses, and spiritual beings, whose help believers seek, and demons, who are feared. Its followers use magic and ritual to harness *te* – virtue or power – in the hope of becoming immortal.

YIN AND YANG
The yin-yang symbol represents the two halves of the Tao, the two opposite, complementary principles Taoists see in nature. Yin is dark, female, passive, soft; yang is light, male, active, hard.

Lu Tung-pin overcame a series of temptations and was given a magic sword, with which he killed dragons and fought evil

Ho Hsien-ku lived on powdered mother-of-pearl and moonbeams; her emblem is the lotus

Li Ti'eh-kuai used to go in spirit to visit Lao-tzu in the celestial regions; he once stayed so long that his body had gone when he came back, so his spirit had to enter the body of a lame beggar

THE FOUNDER
According to Taoist tradition, Lao-tzu lived in central China in the 6th century B.C.E. at the same time as Confucius, who is said to have visited him as a young man. Lao-tzu was a keeper of archives for the Chou dynasty. In later life, tired of Chou corruption, he tried to flee to Tibet. But he was stopped at the border and refused permission to leave unless he left behind a record of his teachings. In three days he produced the *Tao Te Ching,* the greatest of Taoist writings. Then he handed it over and rode away on a water buffalo, never to be heard from again.

Ts'ao Kuo-chiu, patron of the theater, wears a court headdress and official robes, and holds his emblem, a pair of castanets, in one hand

THE EIGHT IMMORTALS
The Eight Immortals are legendary beings believed to have attained immortality, through their practice of the Tao principle. They are said to have lived on earth at various times, and each represents a different condition in life: poverty, wealth, aristocracy, low social status, age, youth, masculinity, and femininity. Here they are shown with a fabulous being called Si Wang Mu, who has the power to give away the peaches of immortality, which grow on the peach tree of the genii, beside the Lake of Gems in the West.

THE FAIRY CRANE
The traditional Chinese focus on death, immortality, and one's ancestors means that funerals, and the rituals surrounding them, are often very important. A paper fairy crane is often carried at the head of the funeral procession of priests (shown here, with the abbot in his chair). The crane symbolizes a winged messenger from heaven, and when the paper crane is burned, the departed soul rides to heaven on the winged messenger's back.

Chang Kuo-lao, a magician, could make himself invisible

> *To exist means to embrace the yang principle (of the light) and turn one's back on the yin (of the dark).*
>
> TAO TE CHING

The magical being Si Wang Mu, here shown as male, more often appears as female

Han Hsiang-tzu is patron of musicians; his emblem is the flute

Lan Ts'ai-ho, patron of florists, holds aloft her emblem, the flower basket

Chung-li Ch'uan holds a fan with which he revives the souls of the dead

GOD OF LONGEVITY
Chinese people see long life as a desirable blessing. Therefore Shou-lai, god of longevity, is a popular deity. He is often depicted, either alone or with the Eight Immortals. His image may be carved in wood and stone, cast in bronze and porcelain, or used as a motif in embroidery and porcelain painting. He is easily identified by his high, bulging forehead and bald head.

RITUAL POWER
Popular Taoism provides for everyday religious needs. Whatever the official philosophy, belief in personal gods and personalized spirits persists, and people still seek their help. Here priests burn incense at a popular ceremony where power (*te*) is harnessed through magic and ritual. Priests are mainly concerned with cures for sickness and disease and with the casting out of evil spirits.

Shinto harmony

SHINTO IS THE MOST ANCIENT religion of Japan. The name means "the way of the gods." It is a religion of nature, focused on *kami*, supernatural spirits, or gods, in which the force of nature is concentrated. Kami include seas and mountains; animals, birds, and plants; even ancestors have the powers of kami. It is said there are eight million kami, worshiped at national, local, and household shrines all over Japan. The force of nature itself is also called kami and is seen as divine. It inspires a feeling of awe and wonder. The most important shrines are associated with places of natural beauty.

SACRED GATE

Since ancient times, Shinto shrines have been marked by entrance gates called torii. Because a beautiful natural setting, such as a sacred open space among trees or rocks, was often sufficient as a shrine, torii stood in such places. The great red torii to the famous island shrine of Itsukushima stands in the waters of the Inland Sea and is one of the great sights of Japan.

SHINTO GODDESS

Kami are rarely represented in the form of images to be worshiped. One exception is Nakatsu-hime, goddess of the Eight-Island Country directly below heaven. In one cult she is seen as an incarnation of the Buddhist goddess Kannon.

The god called Hand Strength Male approaching the cave to bring out the Sun Goddess

The gods decked out the Tree of Heaven with jewels and a mirror, then made music and danced to attract Amaterasu's attention

THE SUN GODDESS AMATERASU

Amaterasu Omikami, the Sun Goddess, is the supreme Shinto god. Her shrine at Ise is the most popular in Japan. One myth tells that her brother the Storm God made her so angry that she hid in a cave, bringing darkness to Earth. To persuade her to come out, the other gods hung jewels and a mirror on the Tree of Heaven and danced for her. She looked out to see what was happening, saw herself in the mirror, and, while watching, fascinated, was pulled outside. Since then, dawn has always followed night.

MOUNT FUJI

Since ancient times, mountains have been seen as special dwelling places of the gods. Much Shinto art deals with sacred mountains, figures, cults, shrines, settings, or themes. Shinto art also reflects the long interaction between Shinto and Buddhism.

HOLINESS

What is "holy" is separate and different, something "other" – far beyond the ordinary. Either beings or places may be holy or sacred. When we experience the holy, we feel awe and wonder, or blessing, or dread, or peace, or a sense of "wholeness." The word "holiness" also refers to moral or spiritual goodness.

SHRINES AND FESTIVALS

Festivals are important in Shinto practice as the time when all a shrine's worshipers focus on the religion. One of the greatest is the Gion Festival, held annually in Kyoto since the 16th century. Local people decorate and wheel tall floats through the streets. During the festival this young boy pays his respects to his local god.

Mallet to grant wishes

Boy taking part in the Gion festival

SHINTO AND BUDDHISM

Shinto is more a religion of experience than of doctrine (set beliefs), so it easily blended with Buddhism after Buddhism reached Japan in the sixth century. The kami were often seen as local manifestations of buddhas and bodhisattvas, and Buddhist temples existed beside, or inside, Shinto shrines. Buddhist monks (such as those above) still take part in the great Shinto festivals.

Wherever the "energy" of the universe attains a particular intensity, revealing itself as beauty, power, wonder, there the ultimate becomes apparent: there is "kami."

FOSCO MARAINI IN *JAPAN: PATTERNS OF CONTINUITY*

The god Daikoku, one of the seven gods of fortune

The god's rat attendant

Sack of rice

THE SEVEN GODS

The seven gods of fortune, or good luck, were originally Buddhist deities and are now worshiped in Shinto, too – another example of how Buddhism and Shinto mix. Daikoku is the god of wealth and patron of farmers. He is often pictured with his son, Ebisu, god of honest labor. Daikoku is usually shown sitting on sacks of rice, with a bag of jewels on his shoulder, a golden sun disk on his chest, and a mallet with which he grants wishes. His attendant is a rat, sometimes shown nibbling away at the rice sacks. Daikoku is rich, though, and always good-humored about the loss of rice. He is also said to be fond of children.

Jain respect for life

JAINISM IS AN ANCIENT INDIAN RELIGION. Its most distinctive doctrine is its belief in *ahimsa*, or nonviolence to living things, which has influenced many non-Jains, including Mahatma Gandhi. Jains believe that the universe has neither beginning nor end – there is no creator god. The universe passes through a never-ending number of cosmic cycles. Each cycle is divided into periods of ascent and descent, during which civilization rises then falls. Tirthankaras (ford-makers) appear; there are 24 in each cycle. They first of all conquer their own passions and emotions, thus liberating and perfecting themselves, and then guide others across the "river of transmigration" (the journey of the soul from one life to the next). Jains believe that the final Tirthankara of the present period was Mahavira, founder of Jainism. Tirthankaras are also called Jinas (conquerors) – the word from which Jains take their name.

Right knowledge comes through keeping the Jain creed, right faith through believing it, and right conduct through following it.

THE "THREE JEWELS"

THE LAST TIRTHANKARA
Vardhamana Mahavira was the 24th and last Tirthankara. Born in the 6th century B.C.E., he was brought up as a prince, but at the age of 28 he gave up everything to seek liberation from the endless round of birth-death-rebirth. He became a beggar and an ascetic (a person who lives a life of self-denial). At about the age of 40 he achieved full enlightenment. He devoted the rest of his life to spreading his beliefs and organizing a community of followers.

TOTAL DETACHMENT
The inner shrine of a Jain temple is dominated by a principal image of the Tirthankara to whom the temple is dedicated. The image is usually flanked by two attendants and surrounded by smaller images of the other 23 Tirthankaras. Here, the 20th Tirthankara sits in passionless detachment for Jains to contemplate.

These diamond- or pear-shaped marks are often shown on Tirthankaras and are good omens

Each Tirthankara has a symbol, in this case the tortoise

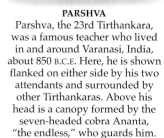

PARSHVA
Parshva, the 23rd Tirthankara, was a famous teacher who lived in and around Varanasi, India, about 850 B.C.E. Here, he is shown flanked on either side by his two attendants and surrounded by other Tirthankaras. Above his head is a canopy formed by the seven-headed cobra Ananta, "the endless," who guards him.

Pilgrims bathing the 60-ft (18-m)-high stone image of the hero Gomateshvara with turmeric

FESTIVALS

Festivals play an important part in Jain life. They may be solemn like Pajjusana, which closes the Jain year, or joyful like Divali, the great Hindu festival that has been adapted in honor of Mahavira's liberation and enlightenment.

DEITIES IN JAINISM

Jains do not worship gods, they contemplate Tirthankaras. That is the theory. In practice, however, many ordinary Jains pray to Hindu deities, and many Jain temples contain images of minor Hindu gods and goddesses. Among the most popular is Sarasvati, goddess of wisdom and the arts.

Sarasvati holds symbolic objects in her hands; the prayer beads in her upper left hand show her piety

The five seated figures around Sarasvati are Tirthankaras

As goddess of wisdom and writing, she holds a palm-leaf manuscript (now broken)

Two fly-whisk holders fan Sarasvati

The two donors are shown kneeling before the goddess

RENUNCIATION

The Jain monk is a homeless wanderer. He owns hardly anything except his robes, pieces of cloth to strain insects away when he drinks, and a brush to sweep insects from the path before him, so as not to crush them.

NONVIOLENCE

Nonviolence, or ahimsa, is the principle of not inflicting harm on others, particularly human beings. For some, particularly Jains, the idea is extended to any living thing. Nonviolence starts with an attitude of mind. It is against harmful thoughts as well as aggressive deeds.

Sikh teaching

Sɪᴋʜꜱ ᴄᴀɴ ʙᴇ ꜰᴏᴜɴᴅ in almost every part of the world. Their gurdwaras (temples) adorn the cities of Great Britain, East Africa, Malaysia, the west coast of Canada, and the United States. The vast majority, however, live in India. Their founder, Guru Nanak, was born in the Punjab in 1469. Nanak taught a new doctrine of salvation, centring on two basic ideas, one about the nature of God, one about the nature of humankind. To Sikhs, God is single and personal. He is the Creator with whom the individual must develop the most intimate of relationships. People are willfully blind; they shut their eyes to this divine revelation and need a guru (a spiritual guide) to teach them. The idea of the guru lies at the heart of the Sikh religion: even the name "Sikh" comes from an old word meaning "disciple." Sikhs recognize 12 gurus: God; Nanak and nine other human gurus, and the 12th guru, the Sikh holy book.

THE SIKH STANDARD
The Sikh emblem, the nishan sahib, contains a ring of steel representing the unity of God, a two-edged sword symbolizing God's concern for truth and justice, and two crossed swords curved around the outside to signify God's spiritual power. A flag with the nishan sahib on it is flown from every gurdwara (Sikh temple).

THE GOLDEN TEMPLE
The Golden Temple at Amritsar is the central shrine of Sikhism and its most important place of pilgrimage. On entering, pilgrims offer coins and each receives a small portion of karah parshad (holy food that symbolizes equality and brotherhood). They then sit and listen to the singing of passages from the scriptures. The water surrounding the temple is considered especially holy and pilgrims often bathe in it.

Silk cloth placed over cover of holy book

FOCUS OF WORSHIP
Gurdwara literally means "the door of the guru," and the temple houses the holy scriptures, called the Guru Granth Sahib. The scriptures contain spiritual poetry written by the ten gurus. The Granth is the supreme authority for Sikhs, and Sikh worship centers on its guidance. The book is greatly revered; it is placed on a cushion under a canopy and covered with a silk cloth in the main body of the temple.

Even when the pages of the Granth are being read, its cover has silk cloths (not shown here) placed over it

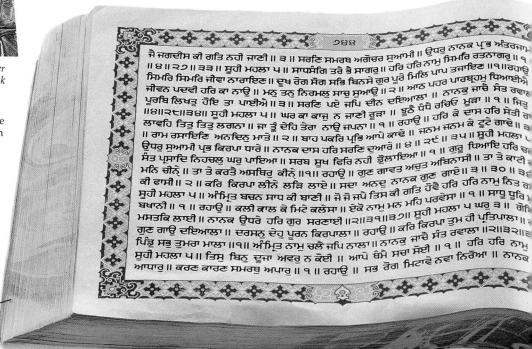

Guru Nanak, founder of the Sikh religion

The kara
(steel bangle)

The kangha
(comb)

THE FIVE K'S
The Khalsa (community) was founded by Gobind Singh, last of the ten gurus. Young Sikhs enter at puberty. It has five outward symbols, known as the "five K's": the sword, comb, bangle, uncut hair (with a turban worn over it), and breeches.

The other nine gurus (shown with halos) sit around Guru Nanak

THE TEN GURUS
Sikhism is sometimes called Gurmat, meaning "the Guru's doctrine." God, the original guru, imparted his message to his chosen disciple, Nanak, first of a series of ten gurus. Gurus were chosen by their predecessors for their spiritual insight. Gobind Singh (1666–1708) was the last. He transferred his authority to the community and the scriptures. He said that the scriptures would be their guru, so the book was called the Guru Granth Sahib.

*God is One,
He is the True Name,
He is the Creator.*

THE OPENING WORDS OF THE *GURU GRANTH SAHIB*

The kirpan
(sword)

The language is a mixture of Punjabi and Hindi and is sung to classical Indian chants; most of the book is poetry

SIGN OF RESPECT
The chauri, or whisk, is a symbol of authority and is waved over the holy book to show honor and respect for it, because a whisk would once have been waved over a human guru in the Punjab (to keep the flies away), and the book is now the guru. The chauri can be made of peacock feathers, yak hair, goat hair, or, as here, synthetic material.

THE GURU GRANTH SAHIB
The Guru Granth Sahib is a collection of the teachings of Guru Nanak and the other gurus. At the beginning are a number of verses attributed to Nanak himself, and these are recited by Sikhs in their morning prayers. Next come poems and hymns that are attributed to various gurus and always sung. Central to the scriptures is the idea of salvation. A Sikh is awakened by the divine guru, and through meditation on the divine Name and hearing the divine Word, the disciple ultimately unites with the divine harmony.

Zoroastrianism

ON THE EXTREME EDGE of the western Iranian desert, in and around Bombay in India, in East Africa, and in many of the major cities of the world are pockets of a small community totaling no more than 130,000 members worldwide. They are the Zoroastrians, known in India as the Parsees, or "Persians," followers of the prophet Zoroaster, who lived in ancient Persia. Zoroaster called for people to live the "good life" and follow Ahura Mazda, the "Supreme Creator," or "Wise Lord," symbolized by fire. Zoroaster believed that the world was essentially good, though tainted by evil. He also believed that, just as Ahura Mazda is responsible for all the good in life, so misery and suffering are the work of an independent force of evil, Angra Mainyu. The two powers are locked in conflict. It is the duty of all people to support the good. Those who choose good are rewarded with happiness. Those who choose evil end in sorrow. Zoroaster taught that in the end good would triumph over evil.

GUARDIAN SPIRIT
Zoroastrians see this image as a fravashi, a guardian spirit. They say that everyone is watched over by a fravashi. Fravashis represent the good, or the God-essence, in people. They help those who ask them and work for good in the universe. This symbol can also be seen as representing "the spiritual self," or Ahura Mazda. It is found very often in Zoroastrianism.

DRINK OF IMMORTALITY
The ritual most associated with Zoroastrians is that of tending the sacred fire. In the major ceremony of Yasna, a prayer ceremony, the sacred liquor haoma (made of the juice of a plant) is offered to the sacred fire. The offering and drinking of this consecrated juice confers immortality on the worshiper.

Mask over face because sacred objects would be contaminated if sneezed on

THE AGE OF RESPONSIBILITY
Before puberty, between the ages of seven and twelve, young Zoroastrians are initiated into their faith in the Navjote ceremony, at which they symbolically take on the responsibility to uphold the ideas and morals of Zoroastrianism. They are given a sacred thread, or kushti, to wear, and a sacred vest, or sudreh. The vest is white, for purity and renewal. The 72 strands of the thread symbolize a universal fellowship.

THANKSGIVING CEREMONY
A Jashan is a ceremony of thanksgiving performed by two or more priests. The officiating priest is known as the zaotar and his assistant as the raspi. Jashan ensures the well-being of both physical and spiritual worlds as the living offer thanks and ask for blessings from the spiritual world. All seven "Bounteous Immortals" (Amesha Spentas), co-workers with Ahura Mazda, and departed virtuous souls are ritually invited down to join the Jashan. The Bounteous Immortals are the guardians of the seven good creations – sky, water, earth, plants, cattle, humans, and fire – represented symbolically by the materials and implements used.

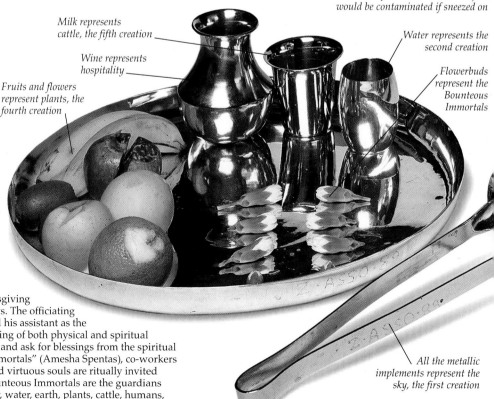

Milk represents cattle, the fifth creation

Wine represents hospitality

Fruits and flowers represent plants, the fourth creation

Water represents the second creation

Flowerbuds represent the Bounteous Immortals

All the metallic implements represent the sky, the first creation

THE FOUNDER

Zoroaster (or, more correctly, Zarathusthra in ancient Persian), is commonly believed to have lived between 1500 and 1000 B.C.E., which would make him the earliest known of the great prophets of the world's religions. Little is known about his life except that he was a priest as well as being a prophet and was married with several children. The religion he founded was for more than a thousand years the official religion of Persia (now Iran), one of the world's greatest empires.

Afarganyu (fire vase); sandalwood burns continuously on it to represent God, the source of light and life

FIRE TEMPLE

Originally, Zoroastrian worship was conducted in the open air. Nowadays, however, every Zoroastrian community worships in a fire temple where prayer rituals are performed in the presence of a sacred fire, which is seen as a living embodiment of Ahura Mazda. No images are allowed, and only Zoroastrians may enter the temple. Before entering, worshipers wash their hands and faces and then perform the kushti prayer ritual. Then they slip off their shoes to enter the fire temple to present themselves before the fire. They apply a pinch of ash from the sacred fire to their foreheads, then pray, focusing on the pure light of Ahura Mazda.

Good thoughts, good words, good deeds.

THE ZOROASTRIAN IDEAL

Tray of sandalwood and frankincense

The traditional oil lamp is kept burning

Flat circular spoon used by the raspi (assistant priest) to offer sandalwood and frankincense to the fire

The Jewish nation

CROSSING THE RED SEA
According to the Bible, the descendants of Jacob's twelve sons, the twelve tribes of Israel, became slaves in Egypt. Eventually, God called Moses to lead them out of slavery. God had to set ten plagues on Egypt before Pharaoh would let them go. Even then, Pharaoh changed his mind and sent his army to trap them by the Red Sea. God parted the sea for the Israelites. When the Egyptians tried to cross, the sea closed over them. This is one of the events commemorated at the Passover ceremonial dinner. The history of the Jewish people is kept alive in their holidays, and the lessons it has taught them about God are remembered.

THE JEWISH PEOPLE trace their ancestry back to three ancient leaders known as the patriarchs: Abraham, his son Isaac, and his grandson Jacob. In their daily prayers, Jews still call themselves "children of Abraham." They call their nation Israel, the name God gave to Jacob. Their story began when Abraham left what is now Iraq about 1800 B.C.E. to settle in Canaan, the "Promised Land," now known as Palestine or Israel. Later, Jacob's sons went to Egypt. Around 1250 B.C.E., their descendants, the Hebrews, were led out by Moses, in the journey known as the Exodus. On the way, the God of the patriarchs appeared to Moses on Mount Sinai and made a covenant (agreement) with Israel. It was enshrined in the Ten Commandments and later in the rest of the Torah, the "Law of Moses." Ever since, this God-given religious law has been at the heart of Israel's identity as a people. Jews see God as both the God of Israel, his "chosen people," and as the Creator and Ruler of all that is, the God who controls history, all-powerful and all-loving.

THE WESTERN WALL
The Western Wall is all that remains of the second Temple, built by King Herod, which stood in Jerusalem 2,000 years ago, when Jerusalem was the capital of the ancient Jewish kingdom. The Temple was the center of Jewish worship until it was destroyed by the Romans in 70 C.E., after which the Jews were scattered and did not have their own state for 1,900 years. The wall is a symbol of the Temple and a memorial of its destruction. It is the holiest site for Jews in Jerusalem.

The Western Wall was called the Wailing Wall because it was associated with crying for the destruction of the temple

Jewish people come from all over the world to pray at the Wall

A BABY BOY
When God made a covenant with Abraham, he commanded that all boys born of Abraham's people should be circumcised as a sign of God's choice of Israel as his chosen people. They are still, to this day, eight days after birth. This is a cloth made for a baby boy.

The Hebrew reads "May he live for the Torah, the huppah, and good deeds"

The huppah, or wedding canopy, the indispensable covering for the bridal pair during the marriage ceremony

The Torah, scroll of the Law

The first part of the
biblical text of the Shema

A ninth candle, called the servant
candle, is used to light the rest

The star of David,
Israel's greatest king

שְׁמַ֖ע יִשְׂרָאֵ֑ל יְהוָ֥ה אֱלֹהֵ֖ינוּ יְהוָ֥ה אֶחָֽד וְאָ֣הַבְתָּ֗ אֵ֚ת יְהוָ֣ה אֱלֹהֶ֔יךָ בְּכָל־לְבָבְךָ֥ וּבְכָל־
נַפְשְׁךָ֖ וּבְכָל־מְאֹדֶֽךָ וְהָי֞וּ הַדְּבָרִ֣ים הָאֵ֗לֶּה אֲשֶׁ֨ר אָֽנֹכִ֧י מְצַוְּךָ֛ הַיּ֖וֹם עַל־לְבָבֶֽךָ וְשִׁנַּנְתָּ֣ם
לְבָנֶ֔יךָ וְדִבַּרְתָּ֖ בָּ֑ם בְּשִׁבְתְּךָ֤ בְּבֵיתֶ֨ךָ֙ וּבְלֶכְתְּךָ֣ בַדֶּ֔רֶךְ וּֽבְשָׁכְבְּךָ֖ וּבְקוּמֶֽךָ וּקְשַׁרְתָּ֥ם
לְא֖וֹת עַל־יָדֶ֑ךָ וְהָי֥וּ לְטֹטָפֹ֖ת בֵּ֣ין עֵינֶֽיךָ וּכְתַבְתָּ֛ם עַל־מְזֻז֥וֹת בֵּיתֶ֖ךָ וּבִשְׁעָרֶֽיךָ

THE MEZUZAH
The mezuzah is a tiny
parchment scroll inscribed
with biblical texts and
enclosed in a case.
Traditionally, mezuzahs are
fixed to the door frames of
Jewish homes. They usually
contain the words of the *Shema*
from the Bible, which calls
God's people to love him
totally. Religious Jews repeat
the *Shema* morning and
evening because it sums
up the heart of their faith.

A candle is lit for each of
the eight days of the festival

*Hear, O Israel: the Lord your
God, the Lord is one....Love
the Lord your God with all
your heart, and with all your
soul, and with all your might.*

THE BEGINNING OF THE *SHEMA*

HANUKKAH, FESTIVAL OF LIGHTS
Hanukkah is an eight-day midwinter festival
marked by the lighting of ritual candles. It
celebrates the rededication of the Temple of
Jerusalem by Judas Maccabaeus after he had
recaptured it from an enemy army in 164 B.C.E.
The Jewish religious year includes a number
of festivals that remind Jews of God's
faithfulness to his people in the past and
help them to be dedicated to him.

JUDAISM	
ONE GOD?	
Yes	
THE AFTERLIFE?	
Yes, but Judaism is mainly concerned with this life	
FOUNDERS?	
Abraham, father of the Jewish people, lived in the Middle East c.1800 B.C.E. Moses, gave the Torah (the Law), lived in the Middle East c.1250 B.C.E.	
SCRIPTURES?	
The Jewish Bible, of which the Torah (the Law of Moses) is the most important part	
A WRITTEN CODE?	
The Torah, which gives guidance for all aspects of life	

People of the Torah

AT THE HEART of the Jewish religion is the Torah, "the Law," written in the first five books of the Hebrew Bible. Torah not only means "law" but also "teaching" and "guidance." In the Torah, God has given teachings about himself, his purposes, and how he wishes his people to obey him in every part of their lives. For a religious Jew, to obey the Torah is to follow God's guidance. The reading of the Torah is a major part of worship in the synagogue (assembly). People also respond to God by communicating with him in prayer. Jewish people believe they have a special role in God's plans for humanity, since it was to them that God revealed the Torah. They look forward to a time when God will send his Messiah ("anointed one") to announce the final setting up of God's rule, or kingdom, on earth.

ARK OF THE COVENANT
The ark of the Law holds the scrolls of the Torah in a synagogue. It sits behind a curtain; facing it, one faces toward Jerusalem. The original Ark of the Covenant held the Ten Commandments while Israel journeyed from Egypt to the Promised Land.

COMING OF AGE
When a Jewish boy reaches thirteen, he becomes Bar Mitzvah, "a son of the commandments." He is then considered to be a responsible adult and is expected to follow all the commandments of the Law. For a girl the age of responsibility is twelve.

The Hebrew text reads "Crown of the Torah"

The crown is a symbol of the Torah because the Torah is seen as the crowning glory of Jewish life

The lion is a common Jewish symbol, originally associated with the tribe of Judah

TORAH AND MANTLE
The European tradition is for Torah scrolls to be kept covered by an embroidered mantle. In the tradition of North Africa and the Middle East, they are kept in a rigid container.

The deeper you dig into the Torah, the more treasures you uncover.

ISAAC BASHEVIS SINGER

SIGN OF RESPECT
A strictly religious Jewish man prays three times a day, in the morning, afternoon, and evening, either at home or in the synagogue. When he prays, he covers his head with a hat or with a skull-cap, known as a yarmulke or kippah. When he goes out, an Orthodox Jew may continue to cover his head as a sign of respect for God.

WEARING THE TORAH
During their daily prayers, Jewish men wear a pair of small black leather boxes containing passages from the Torah strapped to the upper left arm and above the forehead. These boxes are called phylacteries, or tefillin.

CALL TO REPENTANCE
At Rosh Hashanah (the Jewish New Year) the shofar, or ram's horn, is blown to call Jewish people to repentance (to ask God to forgive all the wrong things they have done in the past year). This begins the ten solemn days leading up to Yom Kippur, the Day of Atonement, a day of fasting and repentance, the holiest day of the Jewish year.

Shofar (ram's horn) with Hebrew script on it

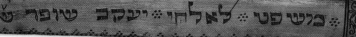

SON OF THE TORAH
When a Jewish boy becomes Bar Mitzvah, the family and community celebrate. They attend the synagogue, and during a Sabbath service the boy will exercise his full adult rights for the first time by putting on the tallit and reading in public from the Law (the Torah) and the Prophets. The tallit is a prayer shawl with tassels at both ends worn by Jewish men at morning prayer and on Yom Kippur. Some, but not all, synagogues also have parallel Bat Mitzvah coming-of-age ceremonies for girls.

The Torah scroll is too sacred to touch, so it is held by handles and a pointer is used to keep the place

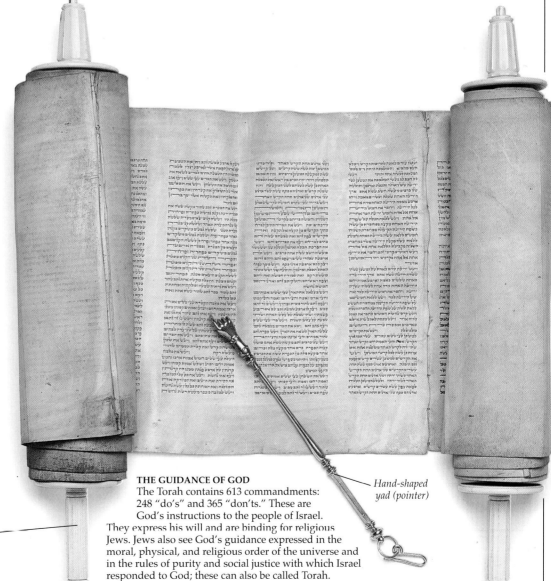

THE GUIDANCE OF GOD
The Torah contains 613 commandments: 248 "do's" and 365 "don'ts." These are God's instructions to the people of Israel. They express his will and are binding for religious Jews. Jews also see God's guidance expressed in the moral, physical, and religious order of the universe and in the rules of purity and social justice with which Israel responded to God; these can also be called Torah.

Hand-shaped yad (pointer)

Family and community

Palm frond

THE CENTER OF JEWISH RELIGIOUS LIFE is the home. Great emphasis is placed on the family and its relationships. The Jewish year contains many festivals, which give a pattern and a rhythm to the community's life. Many of them are not only religious but family festivals too. These festivals bind the community together. They also make the continuing story of Israel's relationship with God a living part of people's lives. The most important is the weekly Shabbat (Sabbath), a day of rest when Jews do no work and recall the completion of creation. At the center of public worship and of social life is the synagogue, or "assembly." On Friday evenings and on Saturday mornings the Jewish community gathers there for Sabbath services.

CUP OF BLESSING
Most Jewish homes have a wine goblet called a Kiddush cup. The name comes from the blessing spoken over the wine and bread during the Sabbath and Passover.

PURIM
Nearly halfway through the Jewish year (in February or March) comes Purim, which is marked by parties where masks and elaborate costumes are sometimes worn. Purim means "lots." The name refers to a time in the 5th century B.C.E. when an official in the Persian Empire called Haman made a plan to kill all the Jews and drew lots to decide when. During the festival, the Book of Esther from the Bible is read aloud to recall how Esther, the King's wife, helped save her people from slaughter.

Purim scroll containing the Book of Esther

Etrog, a citrus fruit

SUKKOT
Sukkot takes place in September or October, at the end of harvest. During this festival, Jews recall how God provided for all their needs when they wandered in the wilderness after leaving Egypt. Festive huts are built, roofed with greenery, and decorated with fruit and flowers. In a ceremony called the "Four Species," a *lulav* is carried in procession with an *etrog* while prayers are said.

Palm, myrtle, and willow are woven together

Lulav, carried in procession at Sukkot

Sukkot huts are built in gardens or next to a synagogue and, if possible, people eat and sleep in them for the week of the festival

LIGHTING THE SABBATH CANDLES
The Jewish day begins and ends at sunset, so the Sabbath, which falls on a Saturday, begins on Friday evening, when the woman of a Jewish household kindles the "Sabbath Lights" and prays for God's blessing on her work and family. The Sabbath table is then laid with bread and wine. Before the meal, the husband praises his wife and recites scriptures about creation and the Sabbath. Then he blesses the wine and bread and passes them around.

PASSOVER

The week-long Passover is the best known of all Jewish festivals. It commemorates the events related in the Book of Exodus in the Torah. The festival is called Passover because, when God sent a final punishment to Egypt to persuade Pharaoh to let his people go, the Angel of Death "passed over" the Hebrews and spared them. At the Passover meal the youngest child in the family asks why this night is different from all other nights. The father tells the story of Israel's deliverance from slavery in Egypt (the Exodus). He tells of the harshness of life in Egypt, of Moses who led the Jewish people out of slavery, of how God gave Moses the Ten Commandments, and how God looked after Israel in the desert.

Egg symbolizes sacrifice

Shankbone of lamb recalls lambs killed at the first Passover

The Haggadah (meaning the "storytelling") is the special order of service for the Passover meal

The word "Pesach," Hebrew for Passover

Cloth with which the unleavened bread (matzoh) is covered when not being eaten

Nut and fruit paste

Vegetable representing spring

Bitter herbs to represent the bitterness of slavery

The special meal held in the home on the first two nights of Passover is called the Seder (order); these dishes are placed on the table to teach the Passover story

Matzoh (bread made without yeast) recalls the haste with which the Israelites left Egypt

Salt water, as a reminder of the tears of slavery

CONTEMPLATION

To contemplate is to think about something or to gaze upon an object. Religious people practice quiet reflection and focused prayer, concentrating their minds on God, or on some other reality that transcends (rises above) the self. By this means they can experience oneness, or "union," with the divine.

The Christian faith

CHRISTIANS TAKE THEIR NAME from Jesus Christ. Jesus was a Jew who lived in the first century in what is now Israel. At the age of 30 he gathered a band of disciples and traveled about, preaching, teaching, and healing the sick. He declared the need for people to repent (ask for forgiveness for their sins) and to believe in and follow him. His disciples saw Jesus as the Messiah the Jews expected. For Christians, Jesus is not just a man. They believe that God, creator and ruler of the universe, became incarnate (came to Earth as a human being) in Christ to offer forgiveness and salvation to humankind. This was necessary, Christians believe, because God is good and people are not, which creates a gap or barrier between humanity and God. Christians see Jesus as the savior (rescuer) who brings people to God.

SIGN OF THE CROSS
Jesus was executed by being nailed to a cross and left to die (this is called crucifixion). The cross later became the main symbol of Christianity because Christians believe that Christ actually brought salvation by his death and resurrection. When people become Christians and are baptized, they are marked with the sign of the cross.

JOHN THE BAPTIST
At the time of Jesus' birth, many Jews were expecting a prophet to come as a "forerunner" heralding the coming of the Messiah. John began teaching before Jesus did, preaching a baptism of repentance for the forgiveness of sins. When Jesus was 30, John baptized him in the River Jordan, after which Jesus began to teach and preach. Christians believe that John came to prepare the way for Jesus, and baptism has always been the sign of a person's entry into the Christian community.

The crown shows Mary as the Queen of Heaven

THE HOLY TRINITY
This picture is used by many Christians to help them think about the Christian belief that God is the Trinity. This means that there are three persons in God – the Father, the Son, and the Holy Spirit – yet at the same time God is one. In the second person of the Trinity, Jesus, God became human. In the third person, the Holy Spirit, God continues to be present on earth.

VIRGIN AND CHILD
Statues of Jesus with his mother, Mary, such as this one, are seen in many Christian churches. Respect for Mary as "Mother of God" has developed steadily in some (though not all) branches of Christianity. She is called "the Blessed Virgin Mary" because Christians believe that Jesus' father was not a man but God. Many Christians have great reverence for Mary and ask her to pray for them from heaven.

CHRISTIANITY

ONE GOD?	Yes: one God in three persons – Father, Son, and Holy Spirit – the Trinity
THE AFTERLIFE?	A final judgment, followed by heaven or hell
FOUNDER?	Jesus Christ, who lived in Palestine c.6 B.C.E.–30 C.E.
SCRIPTURES?	The Bible, made up of the Old Testament (the Jewish Bible) and the New Testament
MAJOR FESTIVALS?	Christmas – Jesus' birthday Easter – His death and resurrection
PRIESTS?	Most denominations have priests

THE CHRISTMAS STORY

The most familiar image of the Christian story is of Christ's Nativity (birth), which Christians celebrate at Christmas. In this picture, Jesus, Mary, and her husband Joseph are surrounded by the animals who lived in the stable, by local shepherds and their sheep, and by angels. The angels are singing "Glory to God in the highest heaven, and on earth peace among those whom He favors" as they rejoice at the birth of Christ, the "Prince of Peace." Jesus was born in Bethlehem in Judea (southern Israel) and brought up in Nazareth in Galilee in northern Israel. His mother, Mary, and Joseph, although poor, were descended from Israel's most famous king, King David.

I am the light of the world. Whoever follows me will never walk in darkness but will have the light of life.

THE WORDS OF JESUS IN *JOHN* 8: 12

Angels announce the birth to surprised local shepherds

God the Father watches from heaven, holding the world in his hand and worshiped by angels

The baby Jesus was born in a stable because there was no room at the inn in Bethlehem

Mary and Joseph are dressed in blue, the color of divinity and heaven

The painting shows the dress and styles of the artist's day

Picture showing the story of Christ's birth, from a 15th-century book

49

Way of the cross

Mary lamenting over the dead body of Jesus

AT THE AGE OF THIRTY-THREE, Jesus was arrested, tortured, and crucified by the Roman authorities who then ruled Israel. Christians believe that as he died, he "took on himself" the sins of everyone (all the wrong and evil that, Christians say, is in us and cuts us off from God) so that anyone could be forgiven by God and live with God forever. Three days later, according to the Bible, he rose from the dead. He appeared to his disciples, then he "ascended" to heaven, returning to his Father. So, for Christians, Christ is a living savior who has defeated death, not a dead hero. They believe that he helps and guides those who follow him and that he makes it possible for all to share in his victory over death and sin.

CUP OF SUFFERING
Shortly before he died, Jesus held a farewell meal, the "Last Supper," with his disciples. He offered them wine to drink and bread to eat and told them to drink from the cup and eat the bread ever afterward, to represent his blood shed and his life laid down for them. Ever since, Christians have followed this command in services called Holy Communion, the Mass, the Eucharist, or the Lord's Supper.

MOURNING MOTHER
At the beginning of the gospel story, Mary is asked if she is willing to be the mother of the Son of God. Her "yes" to God is seen as a great example of faith. Many Christians also see her as uniquely blessed by God. She is not often mentioned in the Gospels, but when the time came for Jesus to die, she was one of the few who did not abandon him. She is often pictured in Christian art. A sculpture or picture showing her mourning over the dead body of her son (as above) is called a pieta.

THE CRUCIFIXION OF CHRIST
Outside the city of Jerusalem, Jesus was put to death with two criminals. He carried the cross on which he was executed to the place of his death. Crucifixion was then a common, very painful method of execution. Christians seek to live, to love, and to accept suffering patiently, as Jesus did, following him in "the Way of the Cross." Pictures of the Crucifixion feature greatly in Christian art. This picture shows people who were said to be there and later Christians together at the foot of the cross, showing that all of them look to the "saving death" of Christ for their salvation.

The pelican was used as a symbol of Christ because it was believed to pierce its own breast to give blood to feed its young

The writing on the cross quotes Jesus as claiming to be "King of the Jews"

One criminal taunted Jesus; the other said, "Remember me when you come into your kingdom"

John, author of the fourth Gospel, whose symbol is an eagle

THE CRUCIFIX AND THE CROSS

Crucifixes show Christ hanging on the cross; they are symbols of his death and the salvation that, Christians say, it brought. Crosses are empty, and so remind Christians of Christ's resurrection. The four Gospels, whose authors are represented on this cross, are the four books in the New Testament that tell of the life, death, and resurrection of Jesus. They are said to have been written by four early Christians named Matthew, Mark, Luke, and John.

Luke, author of the third Gospel, whose symbol is an ox

Matthew, author of the first Gospel, whose symbol is a man

If we have died with Christ, we believe that we shall also live with him.

ST PAUL, IN *ROMANS* 6:8

Lambs were traditionally used for sacrifice; Christ is pictured as the "lamb of God who takes away the sins of the world" because he sacrificed himself

Mark, author of the second Gospel, whose symbol is a lion

RESURRECTION

The body of Jesus was laid in a tomb with a big stone across the entrance. When some of his followers went to the tomb, they found the stone rolled away and the tomb empty. Angels appeared and told them that Jesus had risen from the dead.

ASCENSION TO HEAVEN

After his resurrection, Jesus appeared to his followers in Jerusalem and Galilee over a period of 40 days. He taught them and commanded them to tell all people the gospel ("good news") – that his death had made forgiveness and new life possible for all – and to baptize people in the name of the Father, the Son, and the Holy Spirit. Then he ascended to heaven and returned to God.

The marks of the nails in Jesus' hands and feet are clearly shown in this picture of him rising from his grave

Church of Christ

CHRISTIANS BELIEVE that before Jesus ascended to heaven he promised he would send the Spirit of God to be with his followers after he left them. Shortly afterward, the Holy Spirit descended upon the disciples, who were gathered in Jerusalem, filling them with new boldness and power. They went out and preached that Jesus was the promised Messiah, calling on people to turn away from their sins and be baptized in his name. They formed a community of faith that continues today – an assembly of baptized believers known as "the church," guided by the Holy Spirit. The early church spread rapidly from Jerusalem across the Roman empire. Today it numbers nearly two billion members worldwide. Christians see the church as "the body of Christ," united by faith in him and called to do his work in the world. They seek to love God and other people as Jesus did, to spread his teaching, and to live as he lived.

CHURCH AND CHURCHES
Baptized Christians make up "the church." In today's world there are different branches of the church, and many of the branches are split into different denominations. The buildings in which Christians meet to worship God are also called churches. Church buildings across the world are built in many different ways.

THE SACRAMENT OF BAPTISM
Christians celebrate the two ceremonies of baptism and communion. These ceremonies are called sacraments. (Some Christians believe there are also five other sacraments.) Some branches of Christianity see sacraments as signs symbolizing God's inward, spiritual work; others say they are also instruments used by God to do that work. Baptism is the rite of entry into the church; water is used, symbolizing the spiritual cleansing of the believer's soul.

PETER THE LEADER
Peter was the first disciple to recognize Jesus as the Messiah. He became the chief of the apostles ("sent ones") – the group of 12 leading disciples – and the leader of the early Christians. He is said to have gone to Rome and led the church there.

Peter holds the keys to the kingdom of heaven

Peter is often called the first bishop of Rome

Christians believe the Bible to be "the Word of God"

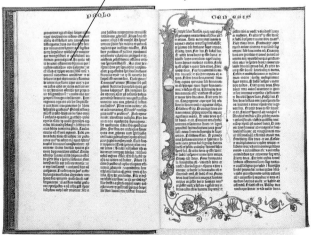

THE BIBLE
The Bible is the Christian holy book. The first part is the Jewish Bible, called the Old Testament by Christians. The second part, called the New Testament, is made up of the writings of early Christians. The Bible is seen as having unique authority.

IHS, the first three letters of the Greek word for Jesus

As a sign of their authority, bishops may carry a staff called a crozier, shaped like a shepherd's crook; this is the head of one such staff

A lamb near a cross, used to represent the sacrifice of Christ

Martin Luther preaching

BISHOPS AND SHEPHERDS

In the Bible Jesus is described as "the good shepherd." Early Christian leaders were therefore also seen as shepherds ("pastors" in Latin), called to look after the people in their churches (the flock) as a good shepherd looks after his sheep. Christians who led and cared for others became known as "pastors" and their leaders as "bishops" (watchers).

PREACHING AND TEACHING

Jesus spent a great deal of time preaching and teaching. He taught both by sermons and by parables – little stories, taken from ordinary life, with a spiritual meaning. The best known of Jesus' sermons is "The Sermon on the Mount," pictured here. Jesus' parables and sermons are recorded in the Bible and are still used today to teach and to spread the Christian faith.

Love the Lord your God with all your heart... and your neighbor as yourself.

THE WORDS OF JESUS, IN MARK 12:30-31

DIFFERENT CHURCHES

By the 11th century, Christianity was split into two main groups: the Roman Catholic church in western Europe, headed by the Pope in Rome, and the Eastern Orthodox, centered on Constantinople (now Istanbul) and eastern Europe. Reformers such as Luther and Calvin broke away from the authority of the Pope in the 16th century, thus creating a third main group. Their followers came to be known as Protestants.

The twelve apostles listen to the sermon

Jesus Christ preaching

The message of Islam

ISLAM IS A RELIGION of submission. Its followers, Muslims, are "those who commit themselves in surrender to the will of Allah" ("Allah" is the Arabic word for God). The word "Islam" itself means "submission" or "surrender." Muslims see their faith as God's final revelation, which meets all the spiritual and religious needs of humanity. The religion began with the Prophet Muhammad, who was born about 571 in the city of Mecca in Arabia. At about the age of 40 he found that he was being called to become a prophet and preach the message of the one true God. At first he met much opposition, and in 622 he left Mecca with his followers for the nearby city of Medina. By 630 he had made them into a powerful religious and political community and was able to re-enter Mecca in triumph.

THE CRESCENT
The crescent, seen on top of many mosques, originally signified the waxing moon. It is associated with special acts of devotion to God. The star and crescent appear on the flags of countries that are mainly Muslim.

SACRED TEXTS
Calligraphy (the art of writing) in Arabic is a great Islamic art. Wherever possible Muslims try to learn Arabic because God revealed his Word to Muhammad in Arabic, and they wish to read it in the original language. The writing on this tile is a fragment from the Koran.

The mihrab in the Gila Khalina mosque

THE KA'BAH AT MECCA
The great mosque in Mecca is built around the Ka'bah (or Kaaba). Set into the wall of the Ka'bah is the Black Stone, which Muslims believe fell from heaven as a sign of the first covenant between God and humankind.

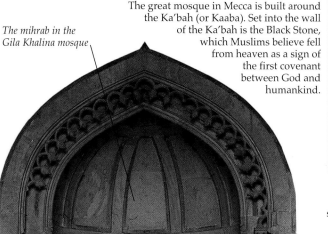

PILGRIMAGE TO MECCA
The Ka'bah is Islam's most sacred site. Every Muslim who is healthy, free from debt, and can afford the journey must make the pilgrimage to Mecca at least once in his lifetime, to visit the Ka'bah and other sacred sites. Pilgrimage is the fifth of the five pillars (or duties) of Islam. The others are: first, confession of faith; second, prayer; third, fasting during the month of Ramadan; and, fourth, charitable giving. The duties are based on the Koran, and the practices of the Prophet Muhammad.

PRAYING TOWARD MECCA
Prayer is the second of the five pillars of Islam. Muslims are required to pray five times a day, facing Mecca: in the morning, at noon, at mid-afternoon, after sunset, and at bedtime. In every mosque there is a niche in the wall, called a mihrab, which faces in the direction of Mecca to show people which way they should turn as they pray.

DOME OF THE ROCK
The Dome of the Rock, with its gilded dome and octagonal base, stands in Jerusalem. After the Great Mosque at Mecca and the Prophet's tomb at Medina, it is Islam's third holiest site. According to Muslim tradition, the rock at its center was the point from which the Prophet Muhammad miraculously visited heaven one night in 619. The site is also sacred to Jews and Christians because the temples of Solomon and Herod stood here.

The words of the shahadah are woven into the curtain covering the walls of the Ka'bah

The Ka'bah is a cubelike building made of gray stone; the Black Stone is set into its eastern corner, on the outside

ISLAM
ONE GOD?
Yes, Allah, the merciful and compassionate
THE AFTERLIFE?
A last judgment, followed by heaven or hell
FOUNDER OR PROPHET?
The Prophet Muhammad, lived in Arabia c.571–632
SCRIPTURES?
The Koran, revealed to Muhammad
PRIESTS?
None
HOLIEST PLACE?
The Ka'bah at Mecca in Saudi Arabia

There is no god but God, and Muhammad is the Prophet of God.

THE SHAHADAH (THE CONFESSION OF FAITH)

People of the Koran

MUSLIMS BELIEVE that the Koran (Qur'an, in Arabic) is the infallible Word of God, expressing God's will for all humankind: final, perfect, and complete. It was revealed in a miraculous way to the Prophet Muhammad, the Messenger of God, who was told to "read" or "recite" the words that were communicated to him by the archangel Gabriel while he was in a trancelike state. "Koran" literally means "recitation." Its central teaching reveals the character of God. Next in importance, it teaches that there will be a last judgment, when all humanity will be raised to life and appear before God to be judged and sent to paradise or hell, depending on one's behavior. It also gives much guidance for behavior here and now. Some of it was revealed in Mecca, and some in Medina after Muhammad's hegira, or flight, to that city in 622. Muhammad began to receive revelations from God in about 610 and continued to receive them until his death in 632. Soon after, these revelations were collected from spoken and written sources to form the Koran.

LEARNING TO RECITE
The Koran is the Muslim's constant companion. From earliest childhood, Muslims hear its words every day. At school, they are encouraged to learn the Koran by heart. Often, they learn to read from its passages.

Believers gathered to hear a sermon being preached

PREACHING
In the mosque the minbar, or pulpit, stands to the right of the mihrab. In early times it had only three steps, but nowadays it is often much more highly decorated and grand in scale, like the one shown here. Only the Prophet Muhammad preached from the topmost step: the imam, or teacher, must take a lower one. Muslims expect to hear a sermon read from the minbar when they gather in the mosque on Friday for midday prayers.

THE ARCHANGEL GABRIEL

When Muhammad was 40, he saw the archangel Gabriel appear before him in human form as he meditated in a cave near Mecca. The archangel spoke the words of God to him. At first, Muhammad wondered if he was imagining this, but soon he sincerely believed that he was hearing God's Word. In the role of divine messenger, he was to retell the words he heard to the Meccans, preach the existence of one God, Allah, and denounce polytheism (the worship of many gods).

THE NAMES OF GOD

The Koran teaches about God by giving him names that describe him, such as Great, Merciful, Keeper, or Guide. In total there are 99 such names. Muslims recite them on 33-bead rosaries and meditate on them. Certain passages, like the famous Throne verse, Surah (chapter) 2.256, inscribed here on a gemstone, describe God particularly eloquently, and at greater length.

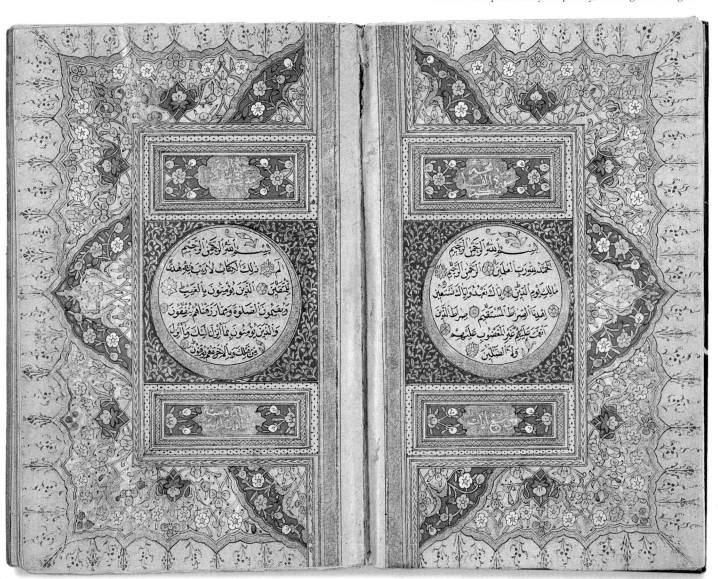

THE KORAN

Muslims believe that the Koran is the last in a series of revelations sent to the world by God that express his will for humankind. The authorized version, written in classical Arabic, was prepared about 650 under Uthman, the third successor to Muhammad. Muslims consider it to be perfect and untranslatable from the original Arabic. The Koran has 114 surahs (chapters). It is often beautifully printed and decorated and may be kept in a special covering or box to show how much it is valued. It can only be touched by Muslims who have first been ceremonially cleansed.

Sultan Baybars' Koran; Baybars was a Turkish slave who rose to rule Egypt and who sponsored the creation of many beautiful objects during his sultanate

O believers, believe in God and His Messenger and the Book He has sent down on His Messenger and the Book which He sent down before.

KORAN 4.136

People of the mosque

FOR MUSLIMS, ISLAM should rule over every part of the life of a person and of a nation, without any distinction between the religious and the rest. The mosque is central to the life of the community, and mosques may be centers for education and social work. The Koran lays down rules to govern not just the life of an individual but also the life of the community. These rules cover all areas of religious and social behavior, from prayer, almsgiving, fasting, and pilgrimage, to marriage, inheritance, and food and drink. Also important are the Hadith (traditions), which record sayings and events in the life of Muhammad and the early Muslim communities. They contain the Sunna (example) of the Prophet – the standard to which all Muslims should aspire. The Koran and Sunna have combined to form the Shari'ah (law), a comprehensive guide to life and conduct, providing a fixed code of behavior for Muslims to follow.

THE POSITIONS OF PRAYER
The above pictures show a Muslim ritually washing himself and then praying. Muslims follow a fixed number of "bowings" while at prayer. There is a set sequence of movements, during which worshipers twice prostrate themselves (that is, kneel, then bow very low with their face to the ground).

CALL TO PRAYER
Five times a day, Muslims are called to prayer by a muezzin, who cries out from a minaret (a tower in a mosque, built for this purpose). Muezzins call in Arabic, beginning with "God is great" and ending with "There is no god but God!"

AT THE MOSQUE
The mosque has an outer courtyard with running water where worshipers perform ritual washings to prepare themselves for prayer. The large inner area is usually covered in carpets and rugs and is unfurnished except for pulpit, lectern, and platform. Here people pray and also hear a sermon at the main weekly service on Friday afternoon.

This mosque, the Badshahi mosque in Lahore, Pakistan, one of the largest in the world, can hold nearly 100,000 worshipers

Worshipers approach the mosque quietly, leave their shoes at the entrance, and ritually wash themselves

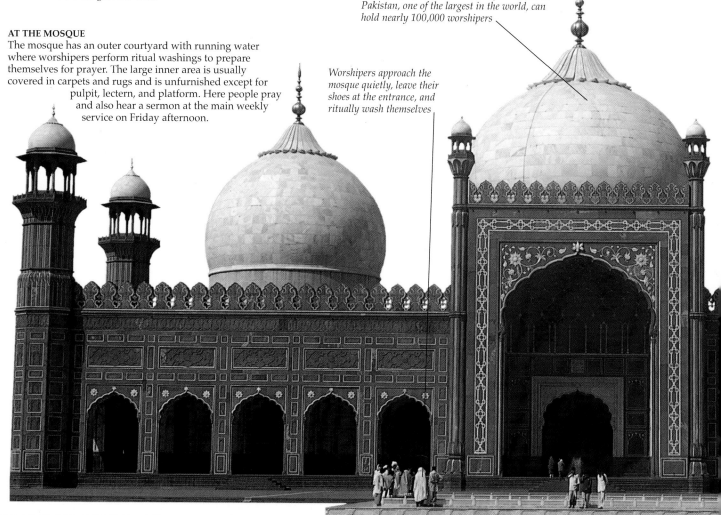

SUFISM

A movement within Islam called Sufism focuses on the direct experience of God. Sufism is found within both branches of Islam, Sunni and Shi'ite. Some Sufis dance as part of their worship. The dancers are popularly known as "whirling dervishes."

Allahu akbar – God is great.

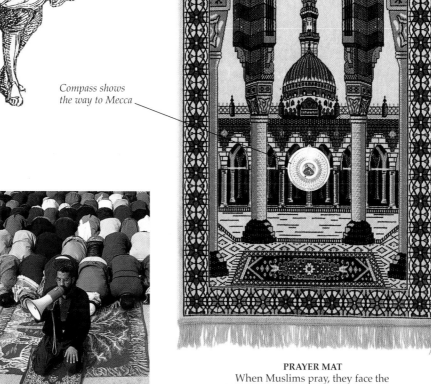

Compass shows the way to Mecca

PUBLIC PRAYERS

These worshipers, led by an imam (religious teacher), are prostrating themselves as they pray. As they bow, they say "Glory be to my Lord, the great." As they prostrate themselves, they say "Glory be to my Lord, the almighty." The megaphone ensures that all worshipers can hear and follow the leader.

PRAYER MAT

When Muslims pray, they face the Ka'bah in Mecca. To find the direction in which to pray, which is called the qiblah, they need a special compass. The compass is an integral part of many modern prayer mats like the one pictured here. Many Islamic countries, such as Iran and Turkey, have a tradition of weaving wonderful carpets and prayer rugs.

Shi'ite standard bearing the names of God, Muhammad, and Ali

SUNNI AND SHI'ITE

Sunni is the majority branch of Islam (90%) and Shi'ite the minority branch (10%). Sunni Muslims see the Shari'ah, made by agreement of the community, as their vital guide, and they believe that after Muhammad's death the caliphs (rulers) who succeeded him were his rightful successors. Shi'ite Muslims believe that only the descendants of Muhammad's daughter Fatima and her husband, Ali, should succeed him. They believe that after Ali died, God sent Imams descended from Ali as his infallible messengers.

The modern spirit

Wɪᴛʜɪɴ ᴛʜᴇ ʟᴀꜱᴛ two hundred years, some less familiar faiths have gained prominence: Some of these, such as the Church of Jesus Christ of Latter-Day Saints, the Unification Family Church, and the Hare Krishna movement, are based on older disciplines, while others, such as Scientology, are completely new. Many new spiritual movements are well respected and are growing in popularity; some, however, attract criticism for their methods of recruitment and the financial workings of their organizations.

SCIENTOLOGY

The main appeal of Scientology is that it sets out very specific practices for spiritual healing and maintains that the salvation of the individual can lead to the transformation of society. Scientology acknowledges the existence of a supreme being, but it does not define his nature, or require its followers to adore or worship him. Similarly, it does not lay down any doctrines that must be accepted blindly.

History
The roots of Scientology lie in the belief of its founder, L. Ron Hubbard, in the relationship between spirit and body. In the early 1950s, he developed a theory called Dianetics, which was intended to show how individuals could rise above emotional, and sometimes physical, damage. Eventually, his theories moved so far into the realm of spirituality that he used them as the basis for a new religion, which he called the Church of Scientology.

Scriptures and beliefs
The writings and lectures of L. Ron Hubbard make up the scripture of Scientology. Followers believe that people lose their spiritual identity through experiences in this life and in previous lives rather than through evil. They claim that humans, who are basically good, have the power to achieve spiritual awareness, solve problems, gain happiness, and accomplish goals. Scientologists see man not as creature with a soul, but as a soul with a body.

Codes and practices
The essence of Scientology lies in two main practices: auditing and training. Auditing is spiritual counseling between a minister and a parishioner, during which the minister asks specific questions, then helps the parishioner to find their own solutions, using a device called an E-Meter. Training involves intensive study of Scientology doctrine, which is believed to deal with all aspects of life. Social consciousness is another important part of Scientology, and many members are involved in their local communities.

L. Ron Hubbard

HARE KRISHNA

Krishna founder A.C. Bhaktivedanta Swami Prabhupada

Hare Krishna is the popular name for the International Society for Krishna Consciousness (ISKCON), part of the Hindu Vaishnava tradition.

History
The movement originated in 16th-century Bengal with the saint Shri Chaitanya, who promoted *bhakti* (loving service to God) and opposed the caste system. His ideas were brought to the West in 1965 by a monk, His Divine Grace A.C. Bhaktivedanta Swami Prabhupada.

Scriptures and beliefs
Krishna theology is based on the Vedas (ancient Hindu scriptures) and related texts. Followers believe in one God – Krishna – but also acknowledge lesser deities. Central to the doctrine is the idea that all living things are spiritual, but each soul forgets this and seeks worldly happiness, taking on successive plant and animal bodies through reincarnation. When a soul reaches the human form, the way it chooses to live determines whether it moves to a lower or higher level. If it is able to revive its love of God, it can break the cycle of birth and death and return to the spiritual realm and an eternal, blissful life of service to Krishna.

Codes and practices
Members regularly chant, study Krishna literature, and practice the system of bhakti yoga. The saffron robes and shaved heads associated with Hare Krisha are attributes of young men training to be monks. Devotees are strict vegetarians who do not take drugs, smoke, or drink tea, coffee, or alcohol. They also abstain from gambling and sex outside of marriage.

CHURCH OF JESUS CHRIST OF LATTER-DAY SAINTS

Mormon Tabernacle, Salt Lake City, Utah

Members of this Church (often called Mormons) are Christians, but they believe that after Christ and his apostles died, the Church drifted away from his doctrine. The apostle Peter prophesied that Jesus would restore his church. Followers believe this process began in 1820, when the prophet Joseph Smith established the Church of Jesus Christ of Latter-day Saints, which follows Christ's original teachings.

HISTORY
Joseph Smith originally founded his church in the state of New York; he was its first president and its first prophet. After his death in 1844, he was succeeded by Brigham Young, who led the congregation to the Great Salt Lake in the present-day state of Utah. Since then, Salt Lake City has been the church's home, and the Mormon Tabernacle there is its international center. Today, Mormon communities thrive in more than 100 countries, with young missionaries regularly traveling the world to share their beliefs.

SCRIPTURES AND BELIEFS
In addition to the Bible, there are three sacred Mormon texts:
* *The Book of Mormon, Another Testament of Jesus Christ*, which relates the story of Christ's visit to ancient America after the Resurrection
* *The Doctrine and Covenants*, a collection of Joseph Smith's revelations and those of his successors
* *The Pearl of Great Price*, Smith's account of the church's founding, and his translation of the record of Moses and Abraham.
Mormons believe that God has restored his church to the earth and that both the Bible and the *Book of Mormon* are the word of God. They also believe in the gifts of tongues, prophecy, revelation, and healing, and in the eventual creation of a "New Jerusalem" in America.
Mormons see the family as the basic unit of both church and society. For a brief time in the 19th century, polygamy was practiced by some Mormons, but it was discontinued by the church before 1900.

CODES AND PRACTICES
The church sets down Christian moral principles, and it particularly encourages service to others. The Mormon health code – the Word of Wisdom – forbids smoking, and drinking tea, coffee, or alcohol.
The church allows members to be baptized after death and revises marriage vows so "till death us do part" becomes "for eternity." Mormons are encouraged to research their ancestry in order to bring as many relatives as possible – both living and deceased – into the church. To help with this, the church has assembled a comprehensive genealogical archive, which is stored in granite caves in Utah.

UNIFICATION FAMILY CHURCH

Although its members are popularly known as Moonies after their founder, the Reverend Sun Myung Moon, this organization is actually called the Holy Spirit Association for the Unification of World Christianity, or HSA-UWC. Moon's book *Divine Principle* teaches that God's original purpose was to establish perfect families that grow and multiply in a perfect relationship with him – a plan confounded by the fall of man but now thought to have found fulfilment in the ministry of Reverend and Mrs. Moon.

HISTORY
Reverend Moon's mission was inspired by a vision of Jesus that appeared to him when he was a teenager in Korea. In 1954 he established the HSA-UWC, and he later set up a number of religious, political, media, and arts organizations to support his ministry. Among these are the Summit Council for World Peace, the International Federation for Victory Over Communism, and the Universal Ballet Company. When his movement reached its 40th anniversary in 1994, Moon declared that it had reached the end of a major cycle, and the current Unification Church would no longer exist.

Claiming that religion had run its course and God would now meet man in the family, he founded the Family Federation for World Peace and Unification (FFWPU) and replaced the old church with the new Unification Family Church.

SCRIPTURES AND BELIEFS
The Bible, the *Divine Principle,* and excerpts from Reverend Moon's sermons form the Unification scriptures. Reverend Moon sees three main problems in the world: absence of morality leading to self-centeredness, the decline of Christianity and the lack of unity among world faiths, and the influence of God-denying doctrines such as Communism. He believes marriage and the family are the only path to salvation.

Unification Family Church mass wedding

CODES AND PRACTICES
Marriage, which takes the form of mass blessings, is the most important ritual in the Unification Family Church. Partners are chosen for members by Reverend Moon, although members are free to reject anyone they consider unsuitable. Couples vow to practice sexual purity and to create a family that lives according to Unification principles and contributes to world peace.

Religious timelines

THESE TIMELINES GIVE a rough comparison of events and developments in the major religions. Because each box covers 250 years, dates can only be approximate, and some dates, such as those in the life of the Buddha, are unknown or disputed. More detailed information can be found in the main section of the book.

Long-running periods, such as the Hindu Vedic period, which extend beyond the range of a single box are marked with an asterisk (*). Names of writings are printed in *italics*.

MEMBERSHIP OF WORLD RELIGIONS

The numbers given here are approximate and intended only as a rough comparative guide. This book does not deal with every existing religion, but extensive information about many more can be found through the Web sites on page 69.

RELIGION	FOLLOWERS	RELIGION	FOLLOWERS
Christianity	1,900,174,000	Sikhism	20,204,000
Islam	1,033,453,000	Judaism	13,451,000
Hinduism	830,000,000	Confucianism	6,334,000
Buddhism	338,621,000	Jainism	3,987,000
Native	96,581,000	Shintoism	3,387,000

	2000–1750 BCE	1750–1500 BCE	1500–1250 BCE	1250–1000 BCE		750–500 BCE	500–250 BCE	250 BCE–CE 1
ANCIENT RELIGIONS	Spread of Celts Egyptian Old, Middle, and *New Kingdoms	Scandinavian Bronze Age	*18th Egyptian Dynasty	Zoroaster, founder of Zoroastrianism	*Fravashi*	Archaic age, Greece Early Rome	Classical Age, Greece *Early Roman Republic	*Hellenistic Age, Greece *Middle and Late Republic, Rome
INDIAN RELIGIONS	*Indus Valley civilization		*Vedic Period	*Brahmanas* (Hindu text)	Mahabharata War (Hindu) Parsva, 23rd Jain tirthankara	Mahavira, 24th Jain tirthankara	Epics and early Puranas (Hindu)	*Bhagavad Gita* (Hindu) Emperor Ashoka (Buddhist)
BUDDHISM			*Student Buddhist monk*	*Jain religious symbol representing peace*		The Buddha First Council at Rajagriha	Emperor Ashoka King Milinda/ Menander *Lotus Sutra*
JAPANESE RELIGIONS				*Tao Yin and Yang symbol*				
CHINESE RELIGIONS	*Hsia Dynasty *I Ching*	*Shang Dynasty		*T'ien-ming/ the Heavenly Mandate *Chou Dynasty	*Spring-Autumn period K'ung Fu-tzu (Confucius)	Lao Tzu (father of Tao)	*Ch'in Dynasty *Former Han Dynasty Confucianism is state religion
JUDAISM	Abraham, Isaac, and Jacob	Moses and the Exodus	Settlement in Canaan	David and the capture of Jerusalem Solomon and the Temple		Second Temple built	Temple extended Herod the Great
CHRISTIANITY	*Islamic tile*						
ISLAM		*Catholic rosary*				

The language is a form of medieval Hindi, which includes words from Persian, Punjabi, and Sanskrit

Standard versions of the Guru Granth Sahib contain 1,430 pages

GURU GRANTH SAHIB
Each religion has its own holy book, and the *Guru Granth Sahib* – also known as the Adi Granth, or primal text – is the sacred scripture of Sikhism. Copies must be treated with great care, so most Sikhs keep a smaller version, the *Gutka*, at home. It contains all the passages used in daily prayer.

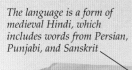

Emperor Augustus

	CE 1–250	CE 500-750	CE 750-1000	1000-1250 CE	CE 1250-1500	CE 1500-1750	CE 1750-2000	
	Height of the Roman Empire	Parsis settle in India					Persecution of Zoroastrians, Iran	**ANCIENT RELIGIONS**
	Vishnu Purana, early *Puranas* *Vaishnavism *Shaivism (all Hindu)	Jain Council at Valabhi	*Vedanta age *Bhakti movement (both Hindu)	*Bhagavata Purana* (Hindu) Bahubali image and shrine (Jain)	Tantras composed		Guru Nanak Amritsar Guru Gobind Singh and the *Guru Granth Sahib*	Mahatma Gandhi Partition of India Hare Krishna	**INDIAN RELIGIONS**
	*Mahayana Buddhism Buddhism enters China	*Tibetan Buddhism Buddhism enters Korea	Buddhism enters Japan *Tantric Buddhism	Buddhism strong in Korea and China	Monk Eisai and Zen Buddhism	Nichiren Bayon Temple, Cambodia	Buddhism restored to Sri Lanka	Chogye Buddhism in Korea Soka Gakkai in Japan	**BUDDHISM**
		Founding of Ise shrine	*Nara period Buddhism in Japan declared state religion	Kojiki and Nihongi compiled (Shinto)	Monk Eisai and Zen Buddhism Dogen and Zen Buddhism	Noh Drama	Original Shinto Motoori Noringa (Shinto)	Nakayama and Tenrikyo Soka Gakkai founded	**JAPANESE RELIGIONS**
	*Hsin Dynasty Latter Han Dynasty Buddhism in China	Chin Dynasty Spread of Buddhism and Taoism	*Sui Dynasty State Buddhism *Tang Dynasty	*The Five dynasties Repression of Buddhism	*Sung Dynasty Confucian revival	*Yuan Dynasty Tantric Buddhism Ming Dynasty	*Ch'ing Dynasty	T'ai Ping rebellion Cultural Revolution	**CHINESE RELIGIONS**
	Temple destroyed Rabbis reconstruct Judaism					Printed prayer book Expulsion from Spain	Ashkenazi and Sephardi communities develop	Hasidism and Zionism Holocaust State of Israel	**JUDAISM**
	Jesus Paul New Testament	St. Patrick in Ireland Fall of Rome	Benedict and monasticism Augustine in England Venerable Bede	Charlemagne Orthodoxy in Russia	First Crusade St. Francis and St. Clare Cistercians and Carmelites	Dominicans Spanish Inquisition	Reformation Loyola and the Jesuits Missions to the New World	Mormons Unification Family Church	**CHRISTIANITY**
			Muhammad Dome of the Rock Sunni/Shi'a divide	Cordoba mosque *Sufism		*Ottoman Empire Capture of Constantinople	Suleyman *Mughal Dynasty Akbar	Islamic Reform End of Caliphate Founding of Pakistan	**ISLAM**

Sikh prayer beads

Jewish seven-branched menorah

Find out more

THERE ARE CENTERS OF WORSHIP for all the major religions in most towns and cities, and most are happy to provide basic information about their structure and beliefs.
For a unique cultural and historical view, however, focus on the ancient city of Jerusalem, the spiritual center of three great faiths: Christianity, Islam, and Judaism. For Christians Jerusalem is the site of Christ's crucifixion, for Muslims it is the place where Muhammad ascended to heaven, and for Jews it is Zion and the City of David. Students of any of these faiths, or of religious history in general, can view more significant sights here than anywhere else on earth. In the nearby Holy Lands are Bethlehem, Christ's birthplace; Mount Sinai, where Moses received the Ten Commandments; and Aqaba, an important stage on the Muslim pilgrimage to Mecca.
Most other faiths have holy sites as well: The Golden Temple at Amritsar, for example, is the center of Sikhism, and the city of Varanasi is sacred to all Hindus.

MADONNA AND CHILD, BETHLEHEM
Custody of the sixth-century Church of the Nativity on the site of Christ's birth is shared by the Roman Catholic, the Armenian, and the Greek Orthodox faiths. This Madonna and Child on display there comes from the tradition of the Greek Orthodox church, which is responsible for the high altar in the Grotto of the Nativity, the building's spiritual heart.

Men and women worship in different areas in front of the wall.

WESTERN WALL
The plaza in front of the holy Western Wall acts as a large, open-air synagogue where Jews from all over the world gather to attend services and pray. Some visitors even write down their messages to God on pieces of paper and tuck them into the cracks between the huge, ancient stones.

GOLDEN TEMPLE, AMRITSAR
The sacred Sikh shrine, or Harimandir ("temple of the Lord") at Amritsar was completed in 1601, but the walls were not given their distinctive gilded-copper finish until the early 19th century. The temple stands in the center of the lake of Amritsar and is linked to the surrounding pavement (*parikrama*) by a 196 ft (60 m) marble causeway.

There are two galleried tiers in the medieval cloister.

LUTHERAN CHURCH OF THE REDEEMER, JERUSALEM
Built for the German Kaiser Wilhelm II in 1898, the Lutheran Church of the Redeemer is situated on the remains of an 11th-century Catholic church, and its many medieval details reflect this. Shown here are the Crusader cloisters, dating from the 13th and 14th centuries and incorporated into the later building.

VARANASI

This entire city on the banks of the holy river Ganges is believed to be a *linga*, an embodiment of the Lord Shiva, as well as his home. The river's waters are thought to be especially purifying here, and Hindus believe that anyone who dies in Varanasi will go straight to heaven, whatever they have done or whatever they believe.

USEFUL WEB SITES

● Kid's site with lots of information about religion. Look for the section where questions about religion are answered by experts: **yahooligans.yahoo.com/School_Bell/Social_Studies/Religion**

● General site that offers an objective overview of six religions – Islam, Hinduism, Christianity, Buddhism, Judaism, and Sikhism: **www.bbc.co.uk/worldservice/people/features/world_religions**

● Directory of Web sites for a wide range of religious organizations: **www.wabashcenter.wabash.edu/Internet/official.htm**

● General site that provides independent surveys of more than 4,200 religions, including statistics, research data, and membership information: **www.adherents.com**

● Survey of sacred places associated with different cultures and religions: **www.sacredsites.com**

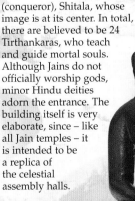

Statue of Parvati, wife of Shiva, at Varanasi

Places to visit

TEMPLE SQUARE, SALT LAKE CITY, UTAH
(800) 537-9703
www.lds.org/placestovisit
This beautifully landscaped 10-acre plot is home to the six-spired Salt Lake Temple, the domed Mormom Tabernacle, and two visitors' centers featuring exhibits and movies relating to the history of the Mormon faith.

THE JEWISH MUSEUM, NEW YORK, NEW YORK
(212) 423-3200
www.thejewishmuseum.org
Founded in 1904, this museum features more than 28,000 objects, including painting, sculpture, photographs, archaeological artifacts, and broadcast media, all of which serve to illustrate the complex nature of the Jewish experience.

WASHINGTON NATIONAL CATHEDRAL, WASHINGTON, D.C.
(202) 364-6616
www.cathedral.org
Built over the course of 83 years and finally completed in 1990, the National Cathedral has been the site of many historic events, such as the funeral of President Dwight D. Eisenhower and the final Sunday sermon of Dr. Martin Luther King. Today, the cathedral continues to open its doors to people of all faiths from every part of the world.

METROPOLITAN MUSEUM OF ART, NEW YORK, NEW YORK
(212) 535-7710
www.met.org
The Met features a huge collection of religious art from around the world. Highlights include the the famous 18th-century Spanish choir screen and nearly 12,000 objects of Islamic art.

VARANASI, INDIA
The most important pilgrimage site in the Hindu faith, Varanasi is also known as Kashi, the City of Light, and, since the period of British rule, as Benares. Pilgrims make offerings to shrines all along the banks of the sacred river Ganges, which is worshipped by Hindus as the river goddess Ganga.

JAIN TEMPLE, CALCUTTA, INDIA
The temple complex, at Sitambar, Calcutta is dedicated to the 10th Tirthankara (conqueror), Shitala, whose image is at its center. In total, there are believed to be 24 Tirthankaras, who teach and guide mortal souls. Although Jains do not officially worship gods, minor Hindu deities adorn the entrance. The building itself is very elaborate, since – like all Jain temples – it is intended to be a replica of the celestial assembly halls.

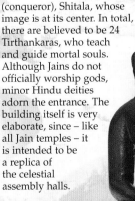

20th Tirthankara

Glossary

Christian angel

AFTERLIFE Life after death

AHIMSA The principle of not inflicting harm on other living things; central to the Jain and Hindu faiths

ANGEL Divine messenger; attendant spirit

ANKH Ancient Egyptian symbol of life; carried only by gods and royalty

APOSTLE Literally "sent one" or "messenger"; one of the 12 men Jesus sent into the world with his message

ASCETIC Someone who practices extreme self-denial and self-discipline, usually for the purpose of spiritual enlightenment. Ascetics often spend their lives in regular prayer and contemplation.

AUDITING Specific form of spiritual counceling practiced in the Church of Scientology

BAPTISM Religious ceremony involving immersion in, or sprinkling with, water as a sign of purification or admission to, a particular church. Baptism is often accompanied by the giving of a new name.

Christian Baptism shown in a Viking illustration

BAR MITZVAH Initiation ceremony for Jewish boys entering adulthood; literally "son of the commandments"

BAT MITZVAH Initiation ceremony for Jewish girls entering adulthood; literally "daughter of the commandments"

BIBLE (*see also* TESTAMENT) Scriptures of the Old and New Testament in Christianity; also used to refer to the scriptures of other religions

CHURCH Can mean either a building used for public Christian worship, the collective body of all Christians, or an organized Christian group such as the Church of Scotland or Church of Jesus Christ of Latter-Day Saints

CREATION Can mean either the act of creating the world or the total of all created things, animate and inanimate

CRESCENT Shape representing the moon in its first or last quarter. The symbol of Islam is a crescent combined with a star.

CROSS (*see also* CRUCIFIXION) Symbol of Jesus Christ's crucifixion, and emblem of the Christian faith

CRUCIFIXION Ancient method of execution that involved nailing a condemned person to a cross and leaving him to die; also, an image of Jesus Christ's crucifixion

DEITY God – either single as in Christianity, or one of many as in the religions of ancient Egypt or Rome

DEMON Evil spirit or devil; destructive supernatural being

DENOMINATION (*see also* SECT) Religious group or sect

DISCIPLE Follower or adherent of a religious leader

DOCTRINE Body of religious, scientific, or political belief

FRAVASHI Guardian spirit in Zoroastrianism. Fravashis represent the good, or the essence of God, in everyone.

GOSPEL Can mean the teachings of Jesus Christ, the record of his teachings in the first four books of the New Testament (Matthew, Mark, Luke and John), or one of these books

GURDWARA Sikh temple; literally "the door of the guru"

GURU GRANT SAHIB Sikh holy scriptures, which contain spiritual poetry written by the ten gurus

Detail of a carved ivory box from ancient Rome that depicts the crucifixion of Jesus Christ

HERETIC Someone who holds an opinion that contradicts religious doctrine

IDEOLOGY Manner of thinking; ideas at the basis of a particular system

IMAM Muslim teacher or prayer leader

IMMORTAL Able to live forever; incorruptible; unfading

INCARNATION Process by which a god takes on bodily – often human – form

KAMI Gods or supernatural spirits in the Shinto faith. Nature, which is seen as divine, is also called kami.

KARMA Destiny or fate; the sum of a person's actions in one life, which, according to Hindu and Buddhist doctrine, determines his or her fate in the following life

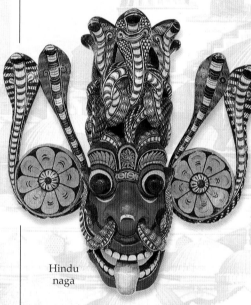

Hindu naga

LAMA Priest in the religions of Tibetan or Mongolian Buddhism

MANDIR Hindu temple or place of worship

MANTRA Devotional incantation, usually repeated many times; particularly associated with Hindu and Buddhist rituals

MEDITATION Religious contemplation that involves freeing the mind of all distracting thoughts

MIHRAB Niche in the wall of a mosque, used to show the direction of Mecca

MINBAR Pulpit in a mosque; stands to the right of the mihrab

MOKSHA Salvation in the form of release from the cycle of rebirth and reincarnation

MONOTHEISM Belief that there is only one God

MORALITY System of principles, ethics and conduct; the degree to which such a system is followed

MOSQUE Muslim place of worship

NAGA Semi-human sacred serpent in Hindu mythology

NIRVANA (*see also* KARMA) In Hinduism and Buddhism, the state of perfect peace and happiness achieved by conquering individuality and desire and gaining freedom from karma

NISHAN SAHIB Emblem of the Sikh faith, consisting of a ring of steel and a two-edged sword, with two crossed, curved swords around the outside

POLYGAMY The practice of having more than one wife (or, less frequently, husband) at one time

POLYTHEISM Worship of many gods rather than one God

PROPHECY Foretelling of future events

PROPHET Divinely inspired teacher or interpreter of God's word; someone who foretells future events

QUR'AN Sacred Muslim scriptures that contain Muhammad's revelations

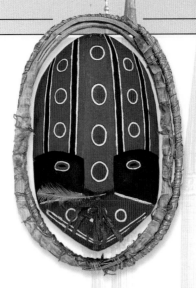

Shaman's mask from Alaska

RESURRECTION Miraculously rising up from a state of death

RITUAL A formal set of religious rites, performed in a certain order

SABBATH Religious day of rest

SACRAMENT Religious ceremony or rite that symbolizes an inner spiritual state. Baptism, marriage, and communion are all sacraments.

SACRIFICE Killing of a living thing, or surrender of a pleasure or possession, as an offering to a god or gods

SADHU (*see also* ASCETIC) Wandering holy man, sage, or ascetic in India

SARCOPHAGUS Elaborate and massive outer stone coffin

SCRIPTURE Sacred religious book or collection of writings

SECT Group of people who follow a particular religious doctrine different from that of the established church from which they have separated

SHAMAN Priest or witch doctor who is able to contact the spirit world

SHRINE Can mean an altar or chapel with special religious associations, or a casket, especially one holding sacred relics

SOUL Spiritual part of a human being that survives bodily death

STAR OF DAVID Figure of two interlaced equilateral triangles that symbolizes the Jewish faith

STUPA Round, often domed, mound or building used as a Buddhist shrine

SUPPLICATION Act of making a humble request to a god or person

Roman sarcophagus

PUJA Hindu rite of daily worship

REBIRTH Spiritual awakening, passing from childhood to adulthood, or moving from death to life; often symbolized by immersion in, or sprinkling with, water

REINCARNATION The belief that we live many different lives on earth, each soul moving into another body after death

RELIC Part of a holy person's body, or item belonging to a holy person, which is kept after his or her death as an object of reverence

SYNAGOGUE Jewish place of meeting for religious observance and instruction; also, a Jewish assembly or congregation

TEMPLE Building dedicated to the worship of a god or gods, or to any other object of reverence; a place is which a god is believed to reside

TESTAMENT Statement of principles and beliefs

THEOLOGY Study of religion; rational analysis of religious faith

TOMB Grave, monument, or building where the body of a dead person is laid to rest

TONGUES Seemingly meaningless strings of syllables uttered spontaneously as part of a religious experience or a service of worship

TORAH The law of Moses, making up the first five books of the Hebrew Bible, traditionally written on scrolls with decorative ends or finials. The word "Torah" means teaching and guidance as well as law.

TRANSMIGRATION (*see also* REINCARNATION) The journey of the soul from one life to the next in the process of reincarnation

TRINITY The Christian concept of one God who exists as three entities or persons: the Father, the Son, and the Holy Spirit

UNDERWORLD In many ancient religions, the place deep under the surface of the Earth where the dead live

VEDAS Early Hindu holy scriptures that are made up of four collections of texts. The Vedas, which were originally transmitted orally, are believed to contain eternal truths.

YIN-YANG Symbol of Taoism consisting of a circle divided into light and dark segments by a curved line; represents the two opposite and complementary halves of the Tao

Jewish Torah scrolls

72-page Eyewitness Titles

American Revolution
Ancient Egypt
Ancient Greece
Ancient Rome
Arms & Armor
Astronomy
Baseball
Basketball
Bird
Castle
Cat
Crystal & Gem
Dance
Dinosaur
Dog
Early Humans
Earth
Explorer
Fish
Flying Machine
Food
Fossil
Future
Horse

Human Body
Hurricane & Tornado
Insect
Islam
Invention
Jungle
Knight
Mammal
Mars
Medieval Life
Mummy
Music
Mythology
NASCAR
North American Indian
Ocean
Olympics
Photography
Pirate
Plant

Pond & River
Pyramid
Religion
Rocks & Minerals
Seashore
Shakespeare
Shark
Shipwreck
Skeleton
Soccer
Space Exploration
Titanic
Tree
Vietnam
Viking
Volcano & Earthquake
Weather
Whale
Wild West
World War I
World War II

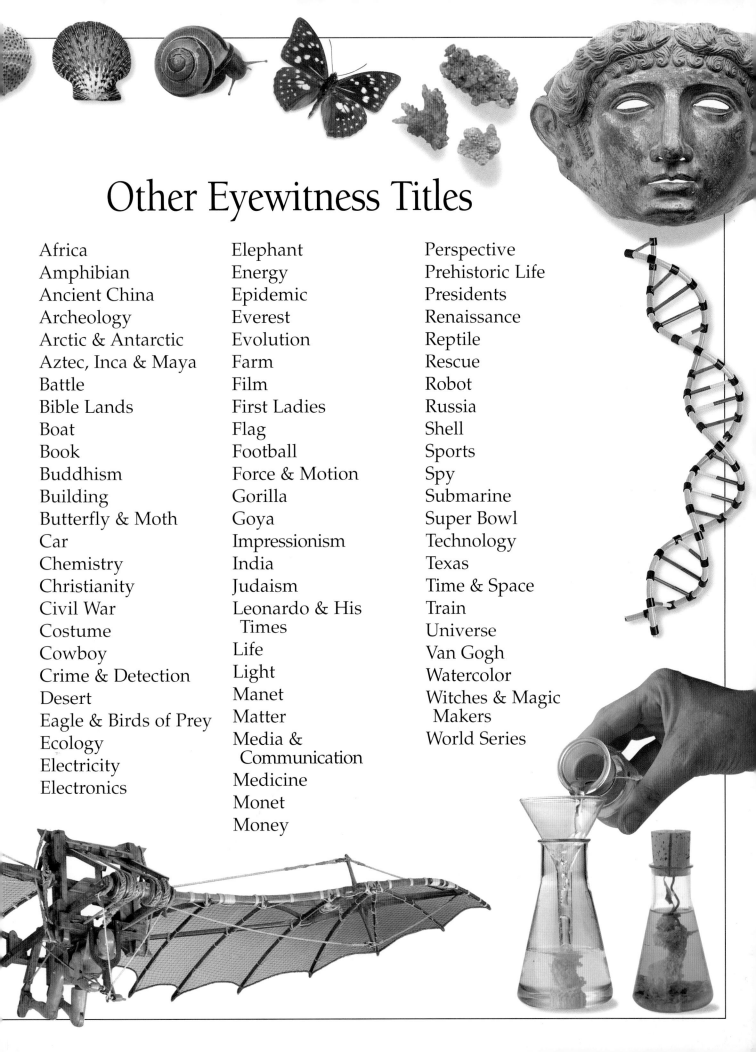

Other Eyewitness Titles

Index

Acknowledgments

The publisher would like to thank:
The Ashmolean Museum (Andrew Topsfield); Surinder Singh Attariwala; The British Museum (Richard Blurton, Dylan Jackson, Graham Javes, Chris Kirby, Jane Newsom); The Buddhapadipa Temple (Venerable Phrakru Lom); The Central London Gurdwara (Bhupinder Bhasin Singh); David and Barbara Farbey; Glasgow Museums (Patricia Bascom, Jim Dunn, Ellen Howden, Antonia Lovelace, Mark O'Neil, Winnie Tyrell); Golders Green United Synagogue (Philip Solomons); Dr. Ian L. Harris, Principal Lecturer in Religious Studies, University College of St. Martin, Lancaster; Professor John Hinnells, Professor of Comparative Religion, School of Oriental and African Studies, University of London; Dora Holzhandler; The Jewish Museum, London (Alisa Jaffa); New World Aurora, Neal's Yard, Covent Garden; The Powell-Cotton Museum, Birchington, Kent (Derek and Sonja Howlett, Malcolm Harman); Dr. John Shepherd, Reader in Religious Studies, University College of St Martin, Lancaster; Indarjit Singh; K. S. Singh; Westminster Cathedral (Father Mark Langham); The Zoroastrian Trust Funds of Europe (Incorporated) (Rusi Dalal).

Artwork: Sallie Alane Reason **Endpapers:** Iain Morris. **Index:** Marion Dent. **Additional photography:** Janet Peckham at the British Museum

The publisher would like to thank the following for their kind permission to use their images:
Picture credits:
(t=top b=bottom c=center l=left r= right)
The American Museum of Natural History, New York (Cat. No. 16/1507): 17bl. **Ancient Art & Architecture Collection:** 55tr, A.S.A.P. / Gadi Geffen: 46bl. **Andes Press Agency:** Carlos Reyes-Manzo 64tl; Peter Grant 64-5background. **Ashmolean Museum**, Oxford: 53tl. **Bridgeman Art Library**, London / Victoria & Albert Museum, London: 21tl, / Bibliotheque Nationale, Paris: 30tl, / British Library: 36tl, 52br, / Giraudon / Musée Condée, Chantilly: Front Cover c & 49, / Oriental Museum, Durham University: 25r, / Osma-Soria Chapter House, Soria / Index: 51bl / Staatliche Museen, Berlin: 13tl, / Staats-und Universitatsbibliothek, Hamburg: 42tl, / Tretyakov Gallery, Moscow: 48c. **British Library:** 52bl, Back Cover bl & 56l. **British Museum:** 4c, 10-11b, 10tr, 10c, 10tl, 11tc, 11tl, 11cl, 12br, 12tl, 12bl, Front Cover

bc & 57tl; 68br, 70bc. **Central London Ghurdwara:** 69t. **Alistair Duncan:** 66bl, 66-7background, 71cl. **E.T. Archive** / National Museum of Denmark: 53tr. **Mary Evans Picture Library:** 20tr, 31bcl, 58tr. **Werner Forman Archive:** 8tr, 34tr; Photographie Giraudon / Musée Condée, Chantilly: 57br, / Musée Guimet, Paris: 24br. **Gables:** 67c. **Glasgow Museums:** 67br, 70cr, 71tc; The Burrell Collection: 13l, 31br, Back Cover tl & 51br, / St Mungo Museum of Religious Life & Art: 15r, © Dora Holzhandler 46br; Sally & Richard Greenhill / Sam Greenhill: 28tl. **Sonia Halliday Photographs:** 12tr, 42c. **Robert Harding Picture Library:** 8tl, 9tl, 16tr, 22tl, 22bl, 26cr, 26tl, 34tl, 38rc, 44tr, 52tr, 54c, 59c. **Hutchison Library:** 14c, / Nick Haslam: 29bl, / Emile Salmanov: 41tr, / Michael MacIntyre: 35tr. **Images Colour Library:** 32bl. **Impact:** / Christopher Cormack: 38lc, / G. Mermet / Cedri: 25tr, / Mohamed Ansar: 22tr. **Jewish Museum:** 71br. **Joods Historisch Museum, Amsterdam:** 44tl; Magnum / Abbas: 56tr, / Bruno Barbey: 8br, 40rc, 40lc, / Fred Mayer: 33br. **Nelson-Atkins Museum of Art**, Kansas City, Missouri (Gift of Bronson Trevor in honor of his father, John Trevor): 30tr. **Christine Osborne:** 64bl, 66tr, 66-7b, 67tl. **Panos Pictures** / Paul Smith:

52cl. **Ann & Bury Peerless:** 37bl, Front Cover lac & 39tl, 58-59b. **Pitt Rivers Museum, Oxford:** 32-33b. **Popperfoto:** 64cl. Reuters 65br. **Peter Sanders:** 54-55b, 54bl, 58tl, 66ca. **Scala:** Florence / Bargello, Florence: 48tr, / Museo di S. Marco, Florence: 50b, 53br, / St Peter's, The Vatican, Rome: 50tr. **Tony Souter:** 70-1background. **Spectrum Colour Library:** 34bl. **Frank Spooner Pictures:** 20tl, Bartholome / Liaison: 37bl; Museum of the Order of St John: 50tl. **Tony Stone Images** / Patrick Ward: 8-9c. **Topham Picture Source:** 30bl. **Trip** / H. Rogers: 38tl. **ZEFA Pictures:** 45cl

Jacket credits:
Front cover: Tl: Kelvingrove Art Gallery and Museum, Glasgow Museums, UK; Tcl: St Mungo, Glasgow Museums, UK; Tc: St Mungo, Glasgow Museums, UK; Tcr: Courtesy of the Ashmolean Museum, UK; Tr: The Burrell Collection, Glasgow Museums, UK; B: © Bill Ross/CORBIS.
Back cover: Bridgeman Art Library, London / New York: cr; Glasgow Museum: bl; Powell Cotton Museum: c.

All other images © Dorling Kindersley.
For further information see: www.dkimages.com